G. W. Cottrell, Jr.
Cambridge
February, 1933

TOURING UTOPIA

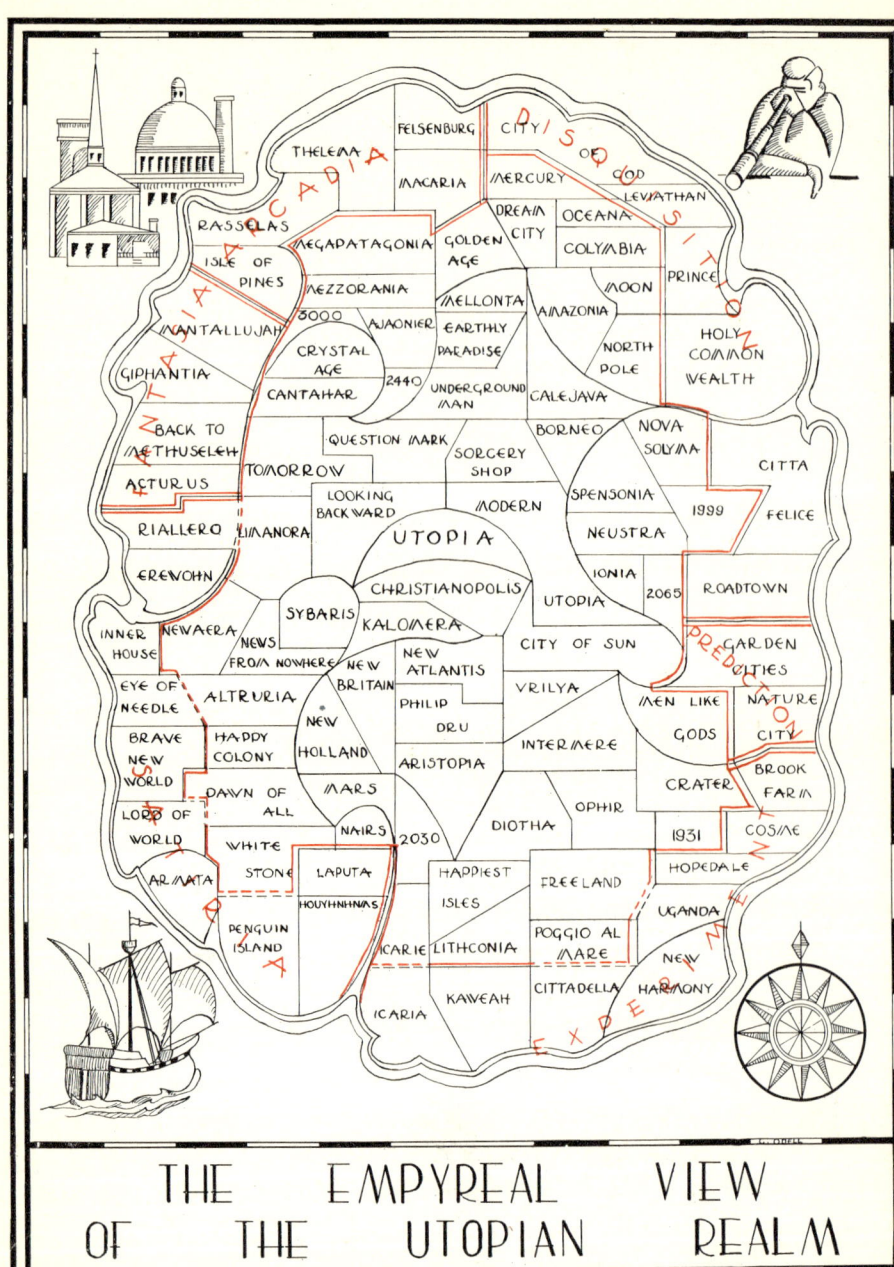

TOURING UTOPIA

The Realm of Constructive Humanism

BY

FRANCES THERESA RUSSELL

*Author of "Satire in the Victorian Novel"
and "One Word More on Browning"*

LINCOLN MAC VEAGH

DIAL PRESS INC.
NEW YORK · MCMXXXII

COPYRIGHT, 1932, BY DIAL PRESS, INC.

MANUFACTURED IN THE UNITED STATES OF AMERICA
BY THE VAIL-BALLOU PRESS, INC., BINGHAMTON, N. Y.

To

MY STANFORD STUDENTS
*who these many years have made for me
the teaching adventure a veritable Utopia*

TABLE OF CONTENTS

		PAGE
PROLOGUE: THE TOURISTS		9
BIBLIOGRAPHICAL NOTE		25

CLASSIFIED LISTS:

I	Utopias Central and Peripheral	27
II	Satiric Utopias and Utopistic Satires	32
III	Specimens from the Suburbs	35
IV	Historical and Critical Treatises	37

CHAPTER

I	PROSPECTUS	41
II	GOVERNMENT	59
III	EDUCATION	84
IV	OCCUPATION	99
V	RECREATION	113
VI	BEAUTY AND ART	125
VII	RELIGION AND MORALITY	136
VIII	DOMESTICITY	151
IX	THE SATIRIC SUBURB	174
X	VERSUS BELLAMY ET AL	203

CONTENTS

CHAPTER		PAGE
XI	THE WORLDS OF H. G. WELLS	235
XII	EXPERIMENTS	252
XIII	SOUVENIRS OF THE TRIP	267
XIV	POSTSCRIPT	281
	L'ENVOI—A. D. 2000	310
	INDEX	311

PROLOGUE

The Tourists

JUST as I was about to start I found myself suddenly and mysteriously companioned. Facing me stood one who was not only a stranger but strange. Yet it was an indefinable oddness. A conventional enough citizen in looks, manner, and, as I soon discovered, speech, he was unmistakably and infinitely foreign.

"May I go with you?" he asked with a directness at once brisk and urbane.

"I shall be glad of company," I replied, "for this excursion I am undertaking promises to be long and lonely. The length does not matter but the loneliness, in a situation that will call for so much question and comment, will be importunate, like an effervescing bottle tightly corked and ready to burst. You seem providential. Are you?"

"That queer term will do as well as another," was his quiet response, "for I can guarantee myself to be a good listener. And my prime asset is that I do not belong to your planet at all."

"Not human?" I cried. "What, then? And, literally, how come?"

He smiled as it were a far-off smile.

"You may identify me merely as a Visitor from Sidereal Space. Cruising around on an exploration of my own, I chanced to spy you about to embark on yours. To accompany you would mean only a short detour for me, and at that not out of line with my general itinerary. And I conceive a mutual benefit out of our temporary travelling fellowship. You can enlighten me as to the inwardness of your human life, and I can assist you to a view of its outwardness."

"By viewing it from a detached and remote standpoint?"

"Just so. The reconstructive effect of an illimitable perspective."

"You are indeed more than welcome," I exclaimed. "I had already been realizing my need of you without knowing of your existence. Now if I had some definite name to call you by I'm sure we could talk like long-lost cronies."

"Since I am an inhabitant of the Empyreal Realm," he replied, "you may call me Empyrean, or, for convenience and easy comradeship, let's say Empy or Emp."

"Thank you. The nickname sounds rather disrespectful, but the whole title is too awesome. To match your handy abbreviation you may address me as Ut,—well, U-t-e, for the long sound."

"Short for Utopian or Utopist, I suppose."

"Not quite, for I am no such thing myself. I am a mere mugwumpian Utopographer, holding no brief for any particular sample of Utopianism but wishing to be intelligent about the whole movement because of its importance as a factor in human civilization. As we gaze into the past we are impressed with the changes that have taken place. As we peer into the future we realize that changes will have occurred. But unfortunately alteration is not always synonymous with improvement. To make it increasingly so by endeavoring to shape the inevitable transformation for better instead of for worse, would seem the a b c of logic, let alone ethics. Only how are we to know what is better and what is worse? Possibly there is no way of knowing. In any case, the only way of reaching a conclusion that is not sheer dogmatic prejudice is by the view both long and wide. Hence my object in planning this very voyage was to get an inclusive squint at our cosmos. Hitherto I have felt as if I were one of the pieces in a patchwork quilt trying to rear up and behold that article's entire surface."

"Or like one leaf on a tree speculating about the branch, trunk, and root of which it is an integral part?"

"You get me. Or, worse yet, like an egg beaten into a cake attempting to visualize the whole compound. We mortals are so sewed into the fabric of life, or grown or stirred or somehow coalesced, that to become an aloof spectator of the altogether is well nigh beyond our ability."

"Except with the aid of imagination."

"Of course it is only through that strange faculty that we are even aware there is anything beyond the physical horizon to see. But our human plight is yet harder than that of these symbolic fractions, for our unit is even less static and permanent. We are plastic actors in shifting scenes on a kinematic stage, all being hurried down the fluid stream of time. Even as we glance, the aspect is otherwise. However zealous we may be to see life steadily and see it whole, we are forced to see it very unsteadily—yes, in our soberest moments—and in scattered fragments."

"And does this Utopia yield more of a whole and steady view?"

"More so, I hope. Anything more than more so, I do not expect. The Utopian looks at life with a comprehensive eye, to be sure, but from an idealistic slant. His creation is a dreamland up above the world so high, but it embodies his notion of what the real world might be if it would."

"Or should be if it could?" amended Emp.

"It's all subjunctive and conditional," I agreed, "but at any rate, it is a whole world in itself, with its own history, geography, psychology, and all the rest. We shall have some trouble, I presume, in making any sort of synthesis or synoptic country out of all its autonomous portions."

"Is it necessary to do so?"

"Only enough to clarify our own impressions and keep us from muddling around too confusedly in the welter. Originally, you understand, each little Utopia was isolated and independent, except for what the later ones borrowed from the earlier, but we may now consider them all as a vast federation, involuntarily allied for our entertainment."

"So what you mean by Utopia is not one or another of these separate entities but the whole extensive and manifold aggregation. Well, Utc, the more there is of it, the sooner we should start. You know the road, I trust, and the way around after we arrive."

"Yes, Emp, I've been poring over Utopian maps, schedules, and Baedekers, off and on, for some time, and have rounded up a bit of equipment, as you see."

"I see: Ethereal biplane, Ithuriel spear, seven-leagued boots, Roentgen ray. Is there nothing for me to contribute?"

"Is that a magic wand I see projecting from your sleeve?"

"Never go abroad without it. Would it come in handy up there?"

"Up there especially it will be well to be invisible.

Only by that trick can we elude the apostolic residents who will be sure to waylay us, take us in charge, show us around, sell us their bright ideas, and make ardent converts out of us after allowing us just enough quavering protest to give a point to our conversion. By doing our own prowling around and collecting our own plunder, we shall be spared from playing up to propaganda. We can investigate according to our preference or judgment, linger or hasten on as we like, retire with our data to some secluded spot, examine our findings ad lib and at our leisure, and vent our opinions on each other."

"Sounds like a plausible program. No harm, is there, in signing our own passports and stealing a march on them this way?"

"It's not really eavesdropping, Emp, merely tuning in, and Utopians are an egregiously broadcasting lot. Besides, if we do walk up and down in their earth and go to and fro in it, it will be not as an Adversary but with an open mind and a cordial spirit. Far from seeking whom we may deflate or what we may devour, we shall be modest and receptive students, asking only to learn."

"That's the typical human attitude, I suppose," said Emp, with a demure grin.

"You embarrass me," I replied, "but I know you are too polite to rub it in. As a matter of fact, I might as well admit that, with all our proneness to prejudice, we are more temperamental over this

PROLOGUE

very Utopianism than almost any other subject. Some give it a fervent embrace, some a pale patronizing smile, some a cold shoulder, and some an angry shove or a vigorous kick."

"Why so vehement? I can see plenty of chances for disagreement over specific details, but who could reasonably oppose the abstract principle of a crystallized idealism?"

"You don't need telling, Emp, that we humans have very little traffic with reason or principles. Any intense objector can pull arguments out of his conscience as triumphantly as a conjuror spills rabbits out of his hat. We shall see them at it later on. One syllogistic line runs somewhat as follows:

All sentimental social reformers are pernicious.
The humanitarian is a sentimental social reformer.
Therefore the humanitarian is pernicious."

"Fallacy of the undistributed middle, isn't it?" mused Emp. "But where does the Utopian come in on this?"

"Oh, he is dragged in as a humanitarian. The two are pronounced one and the same, a thrifty device whereby each one of the Siamese pair may be damned by describing it as the other."

"Fallacy of the unwarranted identification. But even if these terms were synonymous, why shouldn't a human being be a humanitarian? What's wrong with wishing your own race well and trying to make your wishes come true?"

"It might indeed seem that a decent concern for the welfare of the race to which one has the fortune —good or ill—to belong would not be incompatible with other virtues. But according to this cult all virtues are lodged in the humanist, leaving nothing but vices to the humanitarian."

"Why, what's the difference?" cried Emp, arching his eyebrows.

"Difference?" quoth I. "All the difference in the world, sir. In the words of the high priest himself, 'the humanist is opposed diametrically to the humanitarian in being interested in the perfection of the individual rather than in schemes for the elevation of mankind as a whole.' The fresh separation of the sheep and the goats,—and there you are."

"Maybe. But I don't know exactly where I am. Is there a 'mankind' apart from the individuals that compose it? And can any one individual function in a vacuum, hermetically sealed from that aggregation of himself and others known as Society?"

"Most of us do see the individual and his world as mutually interacting factors. We not only grant that the stronger the separate links the stronger the whole chain but we rate that relationship as axiomatic and nothing to make such a fuss about. Humanity may not be a chain-gang but it is in lock-step formation, at least to the extent that any movement is retarded by the weak as well as accelerated by the robust. Our hortatory Humanist himself admits that 'the only direction of drift is toward barbarism,' and that 'civilization is something that must be deliberately willed, first of all by the individual in his own heart.' "

"I'd call that another axiom," said Emp. "But does your discriminating philosopher add the corollary that nothing can be willed until it is conceived and planned? Does he follow up that preliminary 'first' with a developing 'second'?"

"Certainly not, for that process would propel him over into Utopian territory, an obnoxious camp that he wouldn't be caught dead in. One of the many 'menaces to civilization' detected by his probing lance is 'the transformation of the Arcadian dreamer into the Utopist.' That is, as long as this Joseph of the family is content to take it out in dreaming, he is merely that idle fellow and a rather amusing nuisance to have around. But when he starts in telling his dreams and twisting them into prophecies, he must be packed off to Egypt. He has become not merely futile but wicked. However, even in his foreign bondage the young exile dreamed to some purpose and to the ultimate profit of those skeptical and ruthless gentlemen, his brethren, who were not above accepting his life-saving favors."

"And do modern humanistic brethren consistently refuse to take advantage of the material conveniences and scientific appliances that originated as Utopian projects?"

"By no means. Fortunately their antipathies do not extend to the Quixotic self-denial of practising what they preach. In fact, one of the younger disciples of this school names Happiness (the Utopian goal) as the aim of Humanism, and moreover declares the program for achieving that objective as a change of conditions,—'to come out from servitude to things to a command over them'—which is precisely the Utopian method. His phrasing indeed is no more than an echo of one of the despised humanitarians, who says, 'We can retain and transmit our own heritage only by constantly remaking our own environment.' Our allegiance to the past, this philosopher adds, 'is really for the sake of a present so secure and enriched that it will create a yet better future.' That is to say, the Utopian is your only dynamic Humanist. Surely to reassert Man as the measure of all things, natural and spiritual as well as human, and therefore the proper study of mankind, which is good humanistic doctrine, is hardly compatible with ridicule of an interest in this mankind and repudiation of progressive racial evolution, which is the noble creed of our good humanists. More consistent is the identification of an attempt to 'construct, within the world as it is, a pattern of the world as one would have it,' with 'the way of Humanism, in philosophy, in life, and in the arts.'"

"Your last quotation certainly sounds more intelligent," said Emp.

"I can cap that with another which defines intelligence itself as an art of direction which 'consists in the progressive transformation of the present in the light of some envisaged good which it suggests.' At any rate, if our present pagan generation is to adopt Humanism as its revolt from the supernatural and its refuge from the mechanical, it can find a use for the new term *advolution* to supplement the familiar *evolution;* since an unconscious development *out of* becomes humanized by a purposeful unfolding *toward.*"

At this point in our colloquy we had suddenly approached our lofty terminal, for we had meanwhile been winging our way through symbolic space.

"It is not only an immense territory," observed Emp, adjusting his binoculars to the panorama spread out beneath us, "but a mess of subdivisions and uneven in visibility. Some of it lies basking in bright sunlight while other sections are shadowed by clouds or obscured in mist and fog."

"Trailing off, moreover, into contiguous suburbs and provinces, half a dozen of them. The landscape looks like a great wheel with an overgrown hub and short spokes set rather far apart."

"Or like a Gargantuan pie sliced half way to the middle, and the middle itself all carved up into a jumble of districts."

"Yes, those are the individual Utopias, and their respective positions represent their relative purity or adulteration as such."

"How did they get these locations? Did they just grow that way or were they gerrymandered in the interests of some scheme or category?"

"The latter, Emp," I said, "and you were pretty smart to guess it. Assigned seats, as a rule, according to their conformity to the abstract Utopian norm or definition. The most utopian Utopias cluster around the axle, while the more diluted spread away toward the rim. And there they meet the almost-but-not-quites, for the rim itself is a wavering zone rather than a separating barrier. Indeed, what with the insiders clinging to the concave side of the periphery and the outsiders sticking to the convex, it is hard to tell which is which. It is all a confused medley and no simple singleness anywhere."

"Looks to me, Ute, as if we were in for quite a jaunt. I suggest we sit down awhile on one of the suburbs of your solar system and get a little better acquainted with the scenery before we plunge into it."

No sooner said than done, but for a moment the delay promised to be dangerous rather than helpful.

"Astronomy is a fearful thing," I sighed, as Pluto wheeled us in majestic state along his spacious orbit. "I almost wish I hadn't come."

"Don't you find the cosmic view rather comic?" asked Emp, with his cheerfully ironic smile.

"Rather! So comic that it hurts like the tragic. The remoteness necessary for a large view of the whole means no view at all of the details. The distant is small, the small is insignificant, the insignificant is contemptible. Yonder bobbing orange called Earth, merely the third in a row of nine, the whole row merely a straw in the stack, the whole stack merely—"

"Here, here," cautioned Emp, "your cosmos is running away with you. You started to say that little spinning ball could not possibly be carrying a freight of enough importance to deserve a passing thought. What can its picayunish fate matter one way or another? The floating cinder with its swarms of ephemera is doomed to perish sooner or later anyhow. Any civilization it may have evolved will have been perfected only to be destroyed, so what difference does it make whether it had stretched itself to a height of ten millimeters or only seven and a half? The more you consider this ultimate lot, the more mere you feel, and at the same time the more intense your longing to feel less mere. Is that the idea?"

"I'm afraid it is," I admitted ruefully. "Have you any remedy?"

"Of course. The proper antidote for the telescope is the microscope. By its revelations you humans, for all your puny place in the universe, become infinitely large in comparison to the infinitesimally small."

"Well, that at least carries the comfort of relativity. How awesomely immense the meanest of us must look to a mere electron, to whom a microbe is a whale of a fellow! It is the cure by contrasts."

"And also by the realization that the smallest expands to the largest by the most minute gradations. There's nothing either large or small but linking makes it so."

"Thank you, Emp. That means it's worth something for us pygmies to belong to a big universe and have a share in its enormous operations. And after all, it is—wisely—but seldom that we indulge in an orgy of intellectual imagination. As a rule we are emotionally engrossed in our immediate and personal affairs. It is this preoccupation that enables us to snatch a prized and treasured life literally from the very jaws of death."

"And when this saving egoism is assisted by a sense of humor you can see how small you are without feeling small, and thus be steadied without being paralyzed."

"A happy adjustment, Emp. But I fear we'll be paralyzed if we linger here much longer. We should be sufficiently oriented by now to venture the quest. I shall naturally feel more at home in the United States of Utopia than you, but I suppose you are cosmopolitan enough to be easily acclimated anywhere."

"Oh yes, after a fashion. A taste for novelty grows by what it feeds on, and variety of experience is a guaranteed shock-absorber. So I have everything to hope and nothing to dread."

"My own anticipation is no less dispassionate and sanguine. As we tourists thread this mammoth labyrinth we may feel like a couple of Alices in the Looking Glass. For Utopia is a multiple-faceted mirror that reflects a flattering image of the real world—mine, at least—and at the same time by its very distortions casts a sharper light on actuality. By this refraction the proportions, significance, trend and capacities of my mundane sphere should stand forth more clearly delineated."

"Equally true for me, Ute. I'm sure that when we return as travelled Alices from this Wonderland we shall be more alive to the wonders in our own. We may feel no call to adopt or advocate any particular policy or practice, and then again we may become regular salesmen for the new order. But in either event, I agree with you that to bring back heightened perceptions of the values of our home planets, freshened appreciations of their brighter features and greater possibilities, will be to make the trip pay for itself, even if we collect no other mementoes and trophies."

"All right, then," I said, "come on, let's go."

Thus toward the human Eden we took our exploratory way.

BIBLIOGRAPHICAL NOTE

It has been said that a world atlas which does not include a map of Utopia is not even worth looking at. Be that as it may, certainly before such a map can be looked at it must first be made. So far it has been as sketchily charted as the nebulous locales of the Utopias themselves.

Bibliographers and librarians seem to regard Utopia as a convenient No Man's Land into which may be dumped anything that does not belong anywhere else, and some things that patently do, meanwhile excluding certain claimants that really hold cards of admission. Critics and historians of the Utopian tribe make no distinction between twin brothers and fourth cousins by marriage.

Accordingly, for such advantage as a graphic survey may offer, an attempt at symbolic cartography is made in the frontispiece to this volume, the partitioning being further elaborated in the following discussion.

The classified lists are also placed in the beginning instead of being relegated to the usual bibliographical function of bringing up the rear, because some familiarity with them is essential to an understanding of the commentary that constitutes the rest of the report. Frequent reference to these names and dates is the more desirable since the garnering investigator's account of this vast vague chimerical region is laid out along expository rather than narrative lines.

The fact that the Utopian race is still expanding, crowding the yielding plasticity of its borders, makes a complete collection as impossible as a fixed evaluation. After pursuing the quarry into its remotest bookish haunts, after chasing down all suspects (many of which collapsed into quite unutopian frauds), in this design of assembling a practically definitive bibliography, I am now reduced to the chastening realization that of all dreams the Utopographer's vision of a neat taxonomic comprehensive Utopiana is the most Utopian. The latest news is of a forthcoming dissertation, *The Utopian Element in American Literature*, by H. H. Eddy.

However, the list as it stands is doubtless adequate enough to serve as signposts and trails for the interested wayfarer. Any new information or additional items for the collection contributed by fellow tourists in this indeterminate territory of dramatized social idealism will be gratefully received.

F.T.R.

CLASSIFIED LISTS

I

UTOPIAS CENTRAL AND PERIPHERAL

Since the chronological sequence is of primary importance the list is so arranged, with a difference in type to indicate the distinction between the major Utopias—those relatively complete and undiluted—and the minor—those more fragmentary or incidental and thus semi-pseudo, estimated, of course, by the one standard of true Utopianism. Foreign works which have been translated are given their English titles, the others keeping their original form.

CLASSICAL PRELUDE

The Republic, and Critias	Plato
Cyropaedia	Xenophon
Lycurgus	Plutarch

THE MODERNS

1516	UTOPIA	Thomas More
1555	Commentariolus de Eudæmonensium Republica	Gasparus Stiblinus
1619	CHRISTIANOPOLIS	Johann Andreae
1627	THE NEW ATLANTIS	Francis Bacon

CLASSIFIED LISTS

1637 CITY OF THE SUN — Tommaso Campanella
1637 Icaria — Joannes Bisselius
1648 Nova Solyma, or Jerusalem Regained — Samuel Gott
1656 Oceana — James Harrington
1676 Les Aventures de Jacques Sadeur — Gabriel de Foigny
1677 HISTORY OF THE SEVARITES — Denis Vairasse d'Alais
1699 OPHIR — Anonymous
1700 The Adventures of Telemachus — François Fénelon
1700 Histoire de Calejava — Claude Gilbert
1710 Voyages et Aventures de Jacques Massé — Simon Tyssot de Patot
1720 Voyage autour du Pole Boreal — Simon Tyssot de Patot
1727 Le Voyage de Cyrus — Chevalier de Ramsay
1730 La Découverte de L'Empire de Cantahar — Varennes de Mondasse
1737 Gaudentio di Lucca — Simon Berington
1748 Die Gelehrte Republik — Diego Saavedra
1749 DIE GLÜKSELIGSTE INSEL — Ludwig von Faramond
1750 Le Monde d'Mercure — Anonymous
1755 The Center of the Earth — Anonymous
1764 The Cessares — James Brugh
1768 HISTOIRE DES AJAOIENS — Bernard Fontenelle
1772 THE YEAR 2440 — Louis Sébastien Mercier
1781 UN HOMME VOLANT — N. E. Restif de la Bretonne
1795 Spensonia — Thomas Spence
1811 Empire of the Nairs — James Lawrence
1820 NEW BRITAIN — G. A. Ellis
1837 NEW HOLLAND — Mary Fox
1837 Lithconia — Anonymous
1842 LE VOYAGE EN ICARIE — Étienne Cabet

CLASSIFIED LISTS

1842	The Amazonian Republic	Timothy Savage
1847	The Crater	James Fenimore Cooper
1854	The Happy Colony	Robert Pemberton
1865	Anno 2065, Een Blik in de Toekomot	D. Dioscorides
1869	MY VISIT TO SYBARIS	Edward Everett Hale
1871	THE COMING RACE	Edward Bulwer Lytton
1871	The Next Generation	John Maguire
1873	Colymbia	R. E. Dudgeon
1875	By and By	Edward Maitland
1878	Bilder aus der Zukunft	Kurd Lasswitz
1879	The Five Hundred Million of the Begum	Jules Verne
1880	Mars Revisited	Henry Gaston
1881	Three Hundred Years Hence	William Delisle Hay
1883	THE DIOTHAS	Ismar Thiusen
1883	The Dominion in 1983	Ralph Centennius
1883	DIE INSEL MELLONTA	L. B. Hellenbach
1884	History of an Extinct Planet	A. D. Cridge
1887	A Crystal Age	William Henry Hudson
1888	LOOKING BACKWARD	Edward Bellamy
1889	FREELAND	Theodor Hertzka
1890	NEWS FROM NOWHERE	William Morris
1890	The Birth of Freedom	H. B. Salisbury
1891	The Crystal Button	Chauncey Thomas
1891	Looking Beyond	Ludwig Geiseler
1891	The Man from Mars	William Simpson
1892	Mon Utopie	Charles Secrétan
1892	The Future Commonwealth	Albert Chavannes
1893	Shadows Before	Fayette Stratton Giles
1894	The English Revolution	Henry Lazarus
1894	'96, A Romance of Utopia	Frank Rosewater
1894	Young West	Solomon Schindler

1894	Freeland Revisited	Theodor Hertzka
1894	A Journey to Other Worlds	John Jacob Astor
1895	From Earth's Center	S. B. Welcome
1895	Aristopia	Castello Holford
1897	EQUALITY	Edward Bellamy
1897	L'ANNO TRE MILLE	Paolo Mantegazza
1897	Utopie und Experiment	Giovanni Rossi
1898	IONIA	Alexander Craig
1898	LETTRES DE MALAISIE	Paul Adam
1898	The Co-opolitan	F. H. Clarke
1899	The Great Awakening	A. A. Merrill
1900	The World a Department Store	Bradford Peck
1901	INTERMERE	William Taylor
1901	NEUSTRIA	Émile Thirion
1901	Uchronie	Charles Renouvier
1901	Work	Émile Zola
1903	LIMANORA	Godfrey Sweven
1903	DAS IRDISCHE PARADIES	Dmitri Merejkowski
1903	The Case of Theodore Fox	William Stanley
1904	The Dwellers in Vale Sunrise	J. W. Lloyd
1905	A MODERN UTOPIA	H. G. Wells
1905	A Japanese Utopia	Leonard A. Magnus
1905	The White Stone	Anatole France
1905	UNDERGROUND MAN	Gabriel Tardé
1907	THE EYE OF THE NEEDLE	William Dean Howells
1907	In Hundert Jahren	F. E. Bilz
1908	Reciprocity in the Thirtieth Century	Thomas Kirwan
1908	Geyserland	Richard Hatfield
1909	THE SORCERY SHOP	Robert Blatchford
1909	The Lunarian Professor	Anonymous
1911	KALOMERA	W. J. Saunders
1911	The Dawn of All	Robert Hugh Benson
1912	In the Days of the Comet	H. G. Wells

CLASSIFIED LISTS

1912	Philip Dru: Administrator	Edward House
1913	How We Brought about the Revolution	É. Petaud and É. Pouget
1914	The World Set Free	H. G. Wells
1919	Story of the City of Works	F. P. Fairchild
1919	Die Erste Milliarde	Heinrich Ströbel
1920	Democracy—False or True	William Richmond
1920	Doomed	Frank Rosewater
1920	The Dream City	Unitas
1921	The World in 1931	Stewart Bruce
1921	La Révolution du Quatre Septembre	H. L. Follin
1921	Utopie des Îles Bienheureuses	Émile Masson
1922	Der Guterberg	Julius Lerche
1923	MEN LIKE GODS	H. G. Wells
1923	The Golden Age	F. M. Clough
1923	Die Sonnenstadt	Jakob Vetsch
1924	England at the Flood Tide	Kenneth Ingram
1925	La Grande Vague	René Puaux
1926	THE QUESTION MARK	M. Jaeger
1927	TOMORROW	Alfred Ollivant
1927	Man's World	Charlotte Haldane
1929	The Coming Country	Francis Younghusband
1932	The Year of Regeneration	J. C. Lawrence

II

SATIRIC UTOPIAS AND UTOPISTIC SATIRES

1660	The Commonwealth of Oceana	Henry Stubbe
1673	The Floating Island	Richard Head
1705	The Consolidator	Daniel Defoe
1709	L'Île de Naudelay	Anonymous
1725	Memoirs of a Certain Island	Eliza Heywood
1726	Laputa, and The Houyhnhnms	Jonathan Swift
1728	La Nouvelle Cyropedie	Anonymous
1746	Niels Klim	Ludvig Holberg
1763	The Reign of George VI	Anonymous
1813	Utopia Found	Edward Mangin
1816	Armata	Thomas Erskine
1826	The Revolt of the Bees	John Minter Morgan
1828	Captain Popanella	Benjamin Disraeli
1872	Kennaquahair	Theophilus McCrib
1872	Erewhon	Samuel Butler
1880	The Last Days of the Republic	P. W. Dooner
1882	The Fixed Period	Anthony Trollope
1887	The Republic of the Future	Anna B. Dodd
1888	The Inner House	Walter Besant
1890	Looking Further Backward	Arthur Vinton
1891	Pictures of the Socialistic Future	Eugene Richter

CLASSIFIED LISTS

1891	Mr. East's Experiences in Mr. Bellamy's World	Konrad Wilbrandt
1891	Ein Rückblick	Ernst Mueller
1891	Etwas Später	Philipp Laicus
1891	Ein Phantasiestaat	H. E. Erdmansdörffer
1892	Caesar's Column	Ignatius Donnelly
1892	Looking Forward	Richard Michaelis
1893	Looking Within	J. W. Roberts
1894	A Traveller from Altruria	William Dean Howells
1895	The Time Machine	H. G. Wells
1899	When the Sleeper Wakes	H. G. Wells
1900	A Dialogue in Utopia	Havelock Ellis
1901	Riallaro	Godfrey Sweven
1901	Erewhon Revisited	Samuel Butler
1906	The Scarlet Empire	David Parry
1907	The Master Beast	Horace Newte
1907	Lord of the World	Robert Hugh Benson
1908	The Iron Heel	Jack London
1908	Penguin Island	Anatole France
1908	Die Republik des Sudkreuzes	Valerius Bruzov
1910	Newaera	Edward Herbert
1911	The Horroboos	Morrison Swift
1911	Histoire des Quatre Ans	Daniel Halévy
1913	The New Gulliver	Barry Pain
1917	Upsidonia	Archibald Marshall
1918	Meccania	Owen Gregory
1919	Aristokia	A. W. Pezet
1919	Crucible Island	Condé B. Pallen
1924	We	Eugene Zamiatin
1926	The Isles of Wisdom	Alexander Moszkowski
1926	The Sacred Giraffe	Salvator de Madariaga

1927 THE ALMOST PERFECT
        STATE   Don Marquis
1929 MEMORIES OF THE FU-
        TURE   Roland A. Knox
1929 THE SPACIOUS ADVEN-
        TURES   Eimar O' Duffy
1932 BRAVE NEW WORLD   Aldous Huxley
1932 AFTERNOONS IN UTOPIA   Stephen Leacock

III

SPECIMENS FROM THE SUBURBS

Given more or less honorable mention for such Utopian elements as they may have.

TREATISES AND PREDICTIONS

Plato's LAWS
Aristotle's POLITICS
Cicero's DE CIVITATE
Augustine's CITY OF GOD
Patritio's LA CITTÀ FELICE
Machiavelli's PRINCE
Plockboy's VORSCHLAG EINES WEGES
Cornelisson's WAY PROPOSED
Baxter's HOLY COMMONWEALTH
Hobbes's LEVIATHAN
Winstanley's LAW OF FREEDOM
Morelly's CODE DE LA NATURE
Rousseau's SOCIAL CONTRACT
Amersin's IM FREISTAAT
Tarboureich's LA CITÉ FUTURE
Ballanche's LA VILLE DES EXPIATIONS
Schafheitlin's DER GROSSE IRONIKER
Howard's GARDEN CITIES OF TOMORROW
Buckingham's NATURAL EVILS AND PRACTICAL REMEDIES
Rutger's ANNO 1999
Russell's A HUNDRED YEARS HENCE
Mendes's LOOKING AHEAD
Noto's IDEAL CITY
Bucklin's NATURE CITY
Brandt's NEW REGIME
Chambless's ROADTOWN
Tangent's NEW COLUMBIA, or THE RE-UNITED STATES
Flürscheim's DEUTSCHLAND IN HUNDERT JAHREN
Pauer's EUREKANIAN PATERNALISM

Catelani's Nel Mondo del Possibile
Cram's Walled Towns
Francé's Phoebus
Birkenhead's The World in 2030
The Anonymous L'Aurore de la Civilisation

FANTASIES AND ARCADIAS

Virgil's Fourth Eclogue
Sidney's Arcadia
Newcastle's The Blazing World
Rabelais's The Abbey of Thelema
Hartlib's Macaria
Cowley's College
Johnson's Rasselas
The Anonymous Voyage Mystérieux de L'Île de la Vertu
Grivel's L'Île Inconnu
Neville's Isle of Pines
Bretonne's Deux Mille
Schnabel's Die Insel Felsenburg
The Anonymous La Colonia Felice
Mauclair's L'Orient Vierge
Rademacher's Utopia
Ganivet's La Conquista del Reino
Ashbee's The Building of Thelema
Pechmeja's Telephe
Rodney's Star City of Mantallujah
Yelverton's Oneiros
Lindsay's Voyage to Arcturus
Vila's Los Estetos de Teopolis
Tiphagne de la Roche's Giphantia
Phelon's Our Story of Atlantis
Emerson's The Smoky God
Tayler's The Last of My Race
Hauptmann's Island of the Great Mother
Shaw's Back to Methuselah

IV

HISTORICAL AND CRITICAL TREATISES

Excluding socialistic and communistic expositions as well as accounts of cooperative communities in practice.

1855	Staatswissenschaften	Robert von Mohl
1874	Communistische Idealstaaten	Albert Gehrke
1879	Utopias	Moritz Kaufmann
1891	Die Staatromäne	Friedrich Kleinwächter
1892	Schlaraffia Politika	Arthur von Kirchenheim
1894	Toward Utopia	F. H. P. Coste
1897	L'Éternelle Utopie	Arthur von Kirchenheim
1898	Le Socialisme Utopique	André Lichtenberger
1904	Der Idealstaat	E. H. Schmitt
1906	Die Sozialen Utopien	Andreas Voigt
1906	Berühmte Utopisten	Julius Reiner
1911	Französische Utopisten	Emilie Schömann
1913	Der Staatroman des 16 & 17 Jahrhunderts	Joseph Prÿs
1914	Utopie und Robinsonade	Fritz Brüggemann
1921	Moderne Utopien	Rudolf Blüher
1922	The Story of Utopias	Lewis Mumford
1923	The History of Utopian Thought	Joyce Hertzler
1924	Der Utopische Sozialismus	Hans Girsberger
1927	Education in Utopias	Gildo Masso
1929	De Hygiene in Utopia	L. K. Wolff
1929	Ideologie und Utopie	Karl Mannheim

TOURING UTOPIA

CHAPTER I

PROSPECTUS

In spite of the numerous reconnoiterers in the Promised Utopian Land and the zeal and industry of their reports, we are still in some confusion as to its constitution and locality. We do not know exactly what a Utopia is or how it happened or what it is good for or how its protean shape is to be distinguished from its sundry relatives and imitations. The simplest way to find out these things is obviously to start with a definition worked out by the inductive method. If any one member of this Utopian crew could be found to have enough of the constant factors to make it usable as a pattern, the others could be ranked according to their conformity to or divergence from this standard. And by a strange and fortunate coincidence such a model not only exists but it is precisely the one it ought to be. Not because Sir Thomas More invented the name but because he devised the nature is his *Utopia* a satisfactory norm.

The trick of it is deceptively simple. Apparently nothing much happens. A courteous English diplomat sits in a snug Antwerp garden of a serene afternoon along with his guest Peter Giles, and listens to the returned navigator Raphael Hythloday tell of a crescent-shaped island on the other side of the globe. It seems but a casual tale of romantic adventure, an aftermath of the exciting Vespucci expedition, yet it harbors a theory of human welfare considered as a social problem to be solved in a purposeful constructive manner. An ideal is presented in dramatic form, lining up life's main issues as features of a going concern. We hear of a foreign people's daily routine, including such matters as where to live, what to wear, when to eat, how long to work and to play, by whom to be taught, for whom to vote, and under what auspices to worship. But these details are thrown against the screen of an abstract yet practical philosophy. The result is didactic propaganda skilfully woven into a fairly plausible story whose demure air of serving for entertainment only is a transparent mask for the author's persuasive doctrine.

Such is the genus Utopia, but the various species show a wide range of minor diversities. Being of polytheistic creation, amalgamated Utopia is a pluralistic universe whose communes, republics, empires, and anarchies were constructed piecemeal and independently, each one fashioned according to its begetter's vagaries and the style of his time. The general mold may be scientific or artistic or ethical. Some designers insist on simplification;

others revel in decoration. Some put their trust in individualism; others whoop it up for combination. Some provide realistic characters and situations; others strain our credulity with winged men and parallel planets. They express just so many total reactions to life, but each totality is also temperamental and idiosyncratic.

For despite their union in the bonds of speculative idealism the Utopists are a motley tribe. No human enterprise has enlisted greater contrasts in disposition, endowment, and occupation. The authorship roster comprises novelists practiced in narration, statesmen trained in politics, artists and scientists with expert dexterity, and crude amateurs with no equipment save fanaticism for the cause and a honing to impose panaceas. As we encounter their diverse contributions we are now fired with admiration, again absorbed and stimulated, and often vicariously ashamed for the grotesque flimsy junk offered by the incompetent, usually in a spirit of shy apologetic pride. Nothing reveals or betrays a man more than his Utopia, for Utopianism is a test that both taps and traps the human mind.

There are, however, a few distinct lines of cleavage running through the jungle, and one of them is the demarkation between fancy and imagination. To all Utopians wishes are horses, and the eager souls ride hard. But some mount a Pegasus and others a Hobby. Pegasus with a visionary astride becomes an escape mechanism whisking his rider airily to the Never Never Land. Hobby may be spurred by a man of vision to an actual forward movement. He is thus converted into a useful beast of burden, laden with plans and programs and bound for Zion. And the prosaic donkey, laughable as he may be, has this advantage over the poetic steed, that if he ever does arrive he will have gotten somewhere. In fact he has already arrived with a notable baggage of practical schemes and serviceable inventions. As we profit by their ingenuity we have to admit that a Utopia is not of necessity an absurdly outrageous project springing completely panoplied from a slightly demented brain.

It is nearer the truth to say that a Utopia is born whenever a man adds to his dissatisfaction with the terms of his life a formulated proposal of what he would accept as a satisfactory sort of existence. For the Utopian has little right to the halo of disinterested altruism awarded him by the gushing sentimentalists, and even less to the stigma of sentimentality with which he is branded by the current self-styled humanists. He is first and foremost the egocentric rebel. The perfection he craves is a fair and fragrant flower but it is rooted in the heavy black soil of humanity's deep discontent.

Man is primarily the wanting animal—wanting in the double sense of lacking and desiring. As soon as he becomes conscious of this his deprived and longing state he casts about for means of gratifying his tastes and ambitions. The Utopian is convinced that he has the right method. He is anxious to promulgate his recipe for that prime favorite called happiness, though he starts by objecting to his own environment and figuring how it might be improved. It is not that he ignores the improvement of character so emphasized by the humanist but that he considers favorable circumstance a powerful first aid to personal integrity. Things that are means to an end are naturally on a lower plane than things that are ends in themselves, but they are none the less indispensable. The portentous fiat issued by one of the individualistic prophets, that "all things cannot be well unless all men are good," is a double-jointed rule that works both ways, however the elusive term "good" may be defined. And so it is not as a yearning philanthropist but as a shrewd promoter that the Utopian thinks in wholes instead of parts, and translates his program into a universal pattern by the simple device of multiplication. To him humanitarianism is the democratic means of which humanism is the aristocratic end. When the end is achieved the means can be discarded, having become happily superfluous.

Another reason for the apparently greater reliance on external betterment than on self-cultivation is that we mortals have more power over our environment than over ourselves. To say that we can control nature more easily than human nature may have the sound of a paradox but it is a patent enough fact. With nature it is a matter of learning her secrets and outwitting her wherever we cannot secure her cooperation. With human nature it is a matter of a discipline very hard to impose or sustain. The whole human family is a stiff-necked people, inert, stubborn, recalcitrant, not to be coaxed or coerced, even to its own advantage. Nothing then that will help in this job of making a man out of the brute is to be ignored or disdained.

The Utopian also has sense enough to realize that even if he might be content in his selfish heart with a unique and personal perfection and happiness if he could get them, he never could get them. He knows that since no man lives to himself alone the higher level must be spread into a plateau rather than tapered to a row of solitary peaks. His vision is of a coordinated lift from sodden swamp and miasmic jungle to the sunny breezy heights.

The stuff this dream is made of is spun from very ordinary material, the warp gathered from nature, the woof from mankind. The Utopian is one who can take a hint. Beneath the superficial confusion that litters the physical universe he discerns a rigorous structure and an intricate design, testifying to ubiquitous law. In the midst of the human welter he relishes the increasing salvage of order and efficiency. Why continue, he asks, to be tantalized by this glimpse of possibilities? Why view so passively the great discrepancy between life's giant promise and dwarf performance? Why acquiesce in its disgusting failures, weak compensations, and feeble compromises? Why stop with its tiny samples of success? Why not have at the whole murky seething chaos and transform it into a shining symmetrical cosmos and be done with it? As for this being a Quixotic ambition, the artless Spanish Don at least led a more zestful life than is offered either by the dreary treadmill or the inane merry-go-round.

It is not of course that the Utopian has a monopoly on this socially creative ambition. While the bulk of mankind is, to be sure, too benighted or preoccupied or hopeless or short-sighted or anti-humanitarian to be interested in the fate of the world the day after tomorrow, there always has been a minority imbued with these collective concerns, and of this advance guard the Utopians are merely the most vividly expressive branch.

This branch has again two aspects, and these are based not on mood or objective but on manner and a certain technical device employed for the solution of the distance problem.

It is obvious that every Utopia must be at some remoteness, whether great or small, in either space or time; partly to lend enchantment but more to borrow credibility. It is clear also why the earlier productions should specialize on the spatial contrivance, and the later on the temporal. In the days when geography was still in the making and imaginary voyages unhampered by knowledge, Utopians might roam the globe in magic exploration, fancy free. Then the peerless roaming place was the ocean. There was no "unsuspected isle in the far seas." They were all suspected, and the suspicion was readily turned into circumstantial assertion.

Besides the numerous islands thus exploited, two island-continents have received much attention, Atlantis and Australia, the latter being in those days almost as mythical as the former. From the time of Plato's *Critias* to the recent date of Rosewater's *Doomed,* Lost Atlantis has officiated frequently as a Utopian stage. Bacon's *New Atlantis* was moved over into the Pacific, and away down south from there lurked the more magnetic land, the Terra Australis Incognita, rumored long before fully known, where Denis Vairasse, Gabriel de Foigny, and others staked out their Utopian claims.

Of the continents themselves Europe alone was too familiar to provide the requisite mystery. Africa and South America were rich Utopian soil. Asia and North America grew fit Utopias though few. And when the surface of the globe was all used up, there remained the spacious interior.

Entrance to the subterraneous regions was made

through caves or mines or the inflowing current at the North Pole. This last procedure was quite a fad, playing with the notion that the pole literally broke a hole in the earth's crust, through whose opening poured the Polar Sea, sucking with it any vessels abroad in those treacherous waters. But once inside, by whatever means, you found an astonishingly habitable world, sheltered and protected, in pleasing contrast to the appalling exposure suffered by those huddled on the precarious exterior.

In rarer instances the basement of Neptune's domain has been colonized, but it is harder for us to become aquatic, even in imagination. And for some of the most expansive imaginations this little planet, inside or out, is too restricted. These take us on journeys to the moon, to Mars, to Mercury, to a world out beyond Sirius.

That about exhausts the choices of space and forces us to change to the time-machine for transportation. Occasionally this has carried us back to a good old Golden Age but generally its route pushes into the future, a futurity that stretches all the way from the immediately coming years, as in *Oceana* and *Freeland*, to the thirty-second century of *Back to Methuselah*, to the ninety-sixth century of *The Diothas*, to the almost five-hundred-and-third century of *The Last of My Race*. Usually these establishments are finished and flourishing by the time the visitor arrives on the scene, but by way of variety Cooper and Zola and Hertzka describe the process and let us in on the becoming as well as the being.

As a rule the remote in space are contemporary in time, and the distant in time are on the home ground, as Bellamy's future Boston, Thiusen's future New York, Mercier's future Paris, Blatchford's future Manchester, and the future London of Morris, Benson, Wells, Stanley, and Jaeger.

All the while these Utopists have been playing ball with history, tossing the eons back and forth with easy agility, they have been having a history of their own, though the extent to which they have made history is still a question.

This chronicle begins, as the tale is usually told, with a Greek philosopher of the fifth century B.C. or with the Hebrew Prophets of a still earlier date. But those voices crying out to Judah and Israel carried the refrain of protest and warning, lightened only by a fervent faith in an ultimate divine blessing upon a regenerated nation. Their brief impassioned pictures of Paradise Regained, when swords shall be beaten into plowshares, when lions and lambs and little children shall all frolic together, are but beckoning oases of hope over against the vast desert of present despair.

And no more does Plato introduce us to a commonwealth alive and authentic, displaying itself in operation. His conception is dramatized only to the extent of a colloquy wherein the nature of such a political ideal is analyzed and agreed upon—that is, the group obligingly agrees with Socrates. Moreover, the famous Republic was itself something of an accident, a notable instance of the by-product being more valuable than the originally planned product.

After these spasmodic nocturnal blinkings Utopianism evidently decided it had wakened too early and turned over for another nap. With Xenophon's *Cyropaedia* and Plutarch's *Lycurgus* it sleepily opened one eye and then the other. Presently in the Christianized Kingdom of Heaven— the *Apocalypse* revealed by one saint and *The City of God* proclaimed by another—it mingled roseate dreams and sublime expectations. And while thus dozing it was thrown into a coma by the narcotic atmosphere of Medievalism. For that ascetic and scholastic era stooped to no traffic with this world of flesh and deviltry (except to enjoy its feasts and pageantry) and saved all its high anticipation for the blissful destination of all souls (except those reserved for eternal torment) instead of squandering energy on earthly paradises, too carthy at best. But at last, roused by the fresh air and bright sunlight of the Renaissance, Utopianism sprang briskly out of bed and dressed for the day's work.

It was then that the lusty juventus was christened, albeit by a name chosen as a prudent disclaimer. Sir Thomas labelled his creation a Nowhere, saying he could wish rather than hope to see it evolve into a Somewhere. If, however, it should thus materialize, it would no longer be Utopia, No Place, but Eutopia, the Good Place.

Yet even with this auspicious start, Utopia was slow getting under way. Another whole century rolled by before the next manifestation appeared. But after the enterprise once did get up steam it went with a rush, spurting through the seventeenth century, gathering more momentum in the eighteenth, and booming down the nineteenth as the Utopia Manufacturing Company, Unlimited. So far the twentieth has been speeding up in Utopian production to keep pace with its speed in other productions.

During its course its character has become increasingly Eutopian, tending to ignore the helplessly dissatisfied who take refuge in their Fool's Paradise, and approving the dauntlessly unsatisfied who elect to establish their Heaven where it will be of some use, namely here on earth.

If this creative activity were limited to Utopia proper, it would be sufficiently prolific. But it ramifies out into adjoining sections on all sides. From the academic viewpoint Utopia may be pictured as an inner quadrangle, bounded on the north by history and biography, on the east by sociology and economics, on the south by psychology and philosophy, on the west by literature and art. Its arcades open into these various regions and it may be approached from any direction.

More general and adequate to the purpose in hand is the symbolic graph already sketched. These more or less natural affiliations have only the forced relationship of their common association with Utopia. Prediction, Disquisition, Arcadia, Fantasy, Satire, Experiment, form a miscellaneous aggregation not even united to the central realm on the equal terms indicated by our schematic circuit. A stricter metaphor would place the first three on an outer periphery, and sandwich the second three between them and the core.

Prediction includes plain forecasts, bald plans, dry constitutions. Disquisition is an even more barren plateau of exposition and argument. These two are Utopian on the prophetic and sanguine side but are devoid of specific and picturesque elements. Arcadia is the exact opposite, being Utopian in aspect but not in essence. Whether a past Golden Age or a future Millennium, its idyllic Eden was born and not made, a gift of the benevolent gods, not the reward of human providence and initiative. Within its charmed site toil and trouble are not reduced to a decent minimum. They simply do not exist and never did.

Fantasy might seem at first sight less Utopian than its arcadian neighbor, for it is more riotous and bewitched. Yet the very opulence of its Robinsonades and Travelogues makes it rich grazing ground for Utopian fancies, turned out to pasture where they may be free from guiding bridles and restraining fences.

Satire looks on the surface even more alien, since the satirist derives from cynical stock, and the cynic is reckoned as the immemorial opponent of the idealist. But satire is a weapon available for both sides of a conflict, and one which the Utopians themselves have been neither slow in seizing nor awkward in wielding. Moreover, the innately pugnacious satirists are often found fighting among themselves, indulging in mocking masquerades and building little burlesque Utopias. Just as a small actual Utopia may be set in a wide fantastic area, so may scattered satiric dots color the sober Utopian field.

The really diminutive and pathetic patches are in the next territory, the venturesome colonies that had the courage of their convictions, and if they are purple it is only from their bruises. By a mournful irony do these Experiments dwell next door to the specialists in derision, for they themselves constitute a poignantly unconscious satire on the whole reforming industry and its chance of permanent accomplishment.

The last two provinces are of enough consequence to be dealt with later in some detail. At present our survey is to be confined to the central Utopias, and here again we are confronted with the necessity of an artificial segmentation. Since we are interested in the federation as a whole rather than its constituents, we regard it as a unit in order to get at the meaning of its entirety. Yet anything so mammoth and complex must be cross-sectioned somehow, if not from the chronological or biographical angle, then from some other. For this synthetic purpose the most useful principle of subdivision appears to be that of our main human occupations and concerns, the various things we all live by or for or in spite of.

These are best subsumed, as it happens, under the heading of architecture. For wherever man is there are also his buildings, and more than any other one thing they betoken, in their conception and execution, their variety and adaptability, their utility and beauty, the degree of his civilization and the quality of his culture. The Seven Lamps of Architecture collected by Ruskin flickered and scintillated with an uneven amperage but we may, by taking advantage of the coincidence in number, borrow enough of his phrase to light up our own inspection. The Seven Types of Architecture will tell us about all we need to know of Utopia and the actual life out of which it grew.

Since the examination of these representative structures must be made in some sort of order, we shall proceed down—or up—the line from the most public and mechanized of the series to the most private and personalized. The emblematic sequence of these structures, visible to an imaginative gaze revolving around Utopia's unified Civic Center, would unfold itself, let us say, about as follows:

First and foremost stands the Capitol, representing Government as the foundation of all social achievement, in that it has the power either to support and foster or to thwart and hinder the means of associated prosperity.

Next comes the School, providing Education from kindergarten through college, whereby the State's young citizens are equipped for work, directed in play, introduced to laboratory, studio, library, stadium, and all such as samples of human interests.

Then appears the industrial group, Factory, Shop, Office, establishing Occupation to productive ends as the primary fact of existence.

Hardby is the compensating complement, Dancehall and Theater, set in the midst of tennis courts, golf links, ball grounds, skating rinks, and what-not, furnishing Recreation in play as universal as work.

Over against this block and really continuous with it rise the Concert Hall, Opera House, Gallery, Museum, enhanced by an exquisitely landscaped background, expressing the Beauty and Art which

PROSPECTUS 57

are perhaps more purely ends in themselves than any features of life.

Opposite this section and yet correlative are the Laboratories and Research Institutes, witnessing to Truth and Science as supremely vital matters in the advancement of civilization. It happens, however, that they are not treated as separate topics in the ensuing discussion. This omission, it goes without saying, is not due to any lack of importance on their part. On the contrary, Utopia specializes in applied science, basing its whole material structure on its inventions and discoveries, while it makes practical truth, in the form of a rational way of living, its philosophic foundation. But in the actual Utopian operations this truth and this science merge so inextricably into other items that a segregation of them into a chapter of their own does not seem advisable.

Around the corner we see towering in majestic dignity Church and Temple, embodiment of Religion and the Morality that is associated with it, however casual that relationship may be, mayhap cool and strained at times, or even hostile and clashing.

Last but the opposite of least, the Home settles itself in solid comfort, evidence that Domesticity is ingrained in the human constitution, whether sentimentalized, standardized, minimized or emphasized, in its constitution and management.

Yet, although these various factors have their respective places and functions, life diffuses itself through all its housings at will. It calmly ignores all our artificial boundaries and categories. More than that, it keeps dragging influences and reactions from every one of these departments and spreading them around in all the others. This intramural penetration the Utopians are inclined to aid and abet rather than check and counteract.

On the whole they favor the Government of long arm, iron hand, and a finger in every pie; the Education free for all and utilized by all in all activities; Labor and Leisure distributed on the principle of share and share alike; Beauty and Truth permeating everything and never exclusive; eclectic Worship and unanimous Goodness; the Home with no lock on its door and no limit to its hospitality.

But whatever any situation so complicated as the Utopian may be "on the whole," it has all kinds of differences and variations in its component parts. To tell the story of each of these specific enterprises in turn—State, School, Work, Play, Art, Religion, and Family—and how they have fared during the meandering and the torrential course of Utopian history thus far, is the purpose of the next seven chapters. After that, the tale is concerned with certain special points of connection and general considerations.

CHAPTER II

GOVERNMENT

To govern is to exercise authority, to dictate and issue commands, a very jolly and animating employment. But it requires a subject, someone to take dictation and obey commands, a considerably less exhilarating performance. Yet the governed are always the great majority and the governors but few, even in Utopia.

In this idealized world we might expect to find the trend setting decisively toward that freedom which is the desired of all desirers; but the case is just the opposite. Stronger reins are in firmer hands than the *laissez-faire* theory would approve, precisely because the last and least-favored idea to be met with in Utopia is the deflating of public administration. The prevailing type of government is, to be sure, the commonwealth, but that does not mean it is democratic, much less anarchic. And since this institution, like all others, rests on human nature, the explanation is to be sought in psychology.

The reason for government in the first place is a matter of immemorial debate. It may become a

Socratic compromise of interdependence and convenience, or the social contract of Rousseau's hypothesis. But in its genesis there is little of the mutual or the optional. Man is a bundle of feelings and of these the most constant and influential is fear. It is his ignoble destiny to be afraid, and with reason, from the cradle to the grave. To this timorous creature, apprehensive of being hungry or cold, of suffering injury and pain, of not getting what he needs or losing it once obtained, the most precious thing imaginable is simple security. Security is a prize at the disposal of those in power, no matter how they got there. Government as the imposition of external control and the curtailment of personal liberty is only the Oppression side of the medal. The reverse side is Protection.

Advanced as it is beyond this primitive stage, Utopia still has to reckon with elemental conditions. Its development paralleled real life in that the perception of strength in a superior force preceded the discovery of strength in union. Then the principle that in union there is strength had to be vitalized into a policy. Easier said than done. Humans are not naturally cohesive, and are only with difficulty welded into any kind of solidarity. But they are extremely adhesive, and stick tenaciously to any system or practice to which they have become attached.

Being subject in some measure to this force of

habit, the Utopians combine the community life which is their one universal creed with a highly centralized sovereignty. The combination has much to recommend it. The democratic feature is a sop to equity. The autocratic is a device for efficiency.

The ruled are not merely the craven and subdued, and the rulers nothing but despotic tyrants. Even after the multitude became more self-reliant and independent than a flock of sheep bleating for a watchful shepherd and a bunch of faithful dogs to keep the wolves away, it was not averse to retaining a few shepherds to shoulder responsibility and enough dogs to guard its possessions. Homage and tithes it figured a fair price to pay for defense, safety, and the release of time and energy for the prosecution of its private interests.

Another advantage of the efficient regime is its trim and tidy neatness. Often it seems as if the Utopian is more disgusted with the haphazard messiness of ordinary life than with its deprivations and misery. Order is the first law of this heaven, but order means giving orders and receiving and executing them. While of course there is nothing in Utopia to generate unamenables, neither the waywardness of a stubborn disposition nor the provocation of an unjust polity, still we notice that recalcitrant and assertive Lucifers are not present or heard from, and would promptly be pitched out if by accident present and heard from.

For while it is true that only saints should be trusted with autocracy, only angels could prosper in an anarchy; and the Utopians lean with more confidence toward the saintly than the angelic.

Naturally then, the chord sounded in the classic overture by Plato, Xenophon, and Plutarch, is a blend of the three notes: magisterial wisdom, proletarian submissiveness, and a competent hierarchic system. It was justice, to be sure, that Socrates was seeking. But when he fancied he had found it, what did it look like to him? It turned out to be not at all a matter of getting your rights but wholly of accepting your responsibilities. Justice was not a separate virtue but a synthesis of temperance and courage and intelligence, each functioning in its own sphere. Doing your bit and minding your own business operates for the good of the whole, and if you complain that you are not allowed to mind other peoples' business, that you have to mind your own whether you like it or not, and that the chances are against your liking it since it is yours not from your choice but official designation, you are merely betraying an unwarrantable egoism. Plato's eloquent plea for philosophers at the helm and the populace at the oars, clamped to their places if necessary, comes from the focussing of his vision on the Ship of State, a thing of use and beauty, and from his consequent view of crew and petty officers as means to its noble end, not ends in themselves. Hence his ineffable contempt for democracy, lowest level but one in the decline and fall of government.

The completer Utopia that emerged centuries later was a more humanitarian structure erected on the old stable paternalistic foundation. The right of the common people to be well governed did not imply the right to govern themselves. Down to and into the nineteenth century the prevailing sentiment was a mixture of sympathy for the bulk of mankind and distrust of its aptitude for politics. This expressed itself in an indignant protest against cruel exploitation of the helpless and an alarmed protest against undue power being entrusted to their bungling hands.

Sir Thomas More voices the first opinion in the conversation preliminary to Hythloday's story, and the second in the account itself. The Crescent Islanders were flourishing under a system of modified representation. To the early sixteenth century their indulgence in an Electoral College, in Initiative and Referendum, in the Popular Assembly, would seem a daring experiment. Well indeed that the elected prince served for life, that no wire-pulling caucuses were allowed, and that the gathering of an unauthorized assembly was a capital crime. Better still that the daily affairs of the populace were regulated and supervised. Best of all that the citizens were forced to live sober, righteous and godly lives, freed from the cares of personal property and the worries of competitive struggle.

Much the same was the political situation in Campanella's and Andreae's methodical communes, though they had but one city apiece instead of fifty-four. And in contrast to the simplicity and literalness of the German colony, the Italian is picturesque and symbolic. The governing body consists of a Triumvirate—Power, Wisdom, and Love—presided over by the supreme ruler Metaphysics, and assisted by captains of tens and hundreds. Fortnightly assemblies are held for the hearing of popular grievances and for volunteered suggestions, although with Hoh's decisions "the rest are sure to agree." Moreover, no criminal is executed, save for treason or blasphemy, unless he is brought to acquiesce in the justice of his doom. This consent of the condemned is mentioned as the outcome of having but few laws and no dead-letters.

Campanella's low opinion of The People as "a beast of muddy brain," was foreshadowed by the aristocratic fantasy of Gaspar Stiblimus, centered in Eudaemon, the Capital of Macaria Island; and echoed by Bacon's frank confession that he "did not love the word People." Harrington's recognition that "the People can feel although they cannot think," sums up the whole persistent policy of benevolent autocracy. In accordance with this compromise the earlier Utopias are described as founded by some wise benign demi-god; proletariat revolutions are a recent invention. As the old Atlantis was established by Poseidon, and mighty curses invoked upon the disobedient, so was Salomana the original law-giver for the new Atlantis in the Northern Pacific. And the latter's kind but firm dispensation started about the time the pioneer Utopus was conquering and saving the savage Abraxa, in the fourth century B.C.

The South Sea paradise of Vairasse d'Alais was ruled by Prince Sevarminus, the 7509th descendant from the King Severias who inaugurated the idyllic regime. This State took possession of all children from their eighth year, and banished all deformed or troublesome characters. In the same vicinity Gabriel de Foigny's traveller, Jacques Sadeur, discovered a community so peaceful that no one died except of ennui, yet so well disciplined that no one dared thus eat from the Tree of Rest unless he were a centenarian or mortally wounded, and then only after he had provided a substitute at least thirty-six years of age.

Sterner and stricter than any of these is the Teutonic ideal, "Der Wohleingerichtete Staat des bishero von vielen gesuchten aber night gefundenen Königreichs Ophir," founded long ago by King Zadiack and now presided over by a most exemplary monarch, his worthy spouse, and a dignified court, regal without extravagance. The throne is hereditary in that the crown prince is the preferred candidate but not guaranteed of election by the patrician voting body. Part of the coronation oath is a promise not to enlarge the domain by military conquests. The citizens are industrious, thrifty, and peaceable, willy-nilly, being prohibited from profiteering, gambling, Sabbath-breaking, and all forms of luxury. Owners of uncultivated land and game preserves are taxed to the amount of the ground's potential productivity. Prices are controlled, storage for crops provided, standards required of all manufactured goods, and pure-food laws enforced. Yet these drastic regulations are kept flexible by constant scrutiny and official debates on methods of improvement.

Although the English *Oceana* was projected nearly half a century earlier, it shows the liberalizing influence of its political background. Its author declared his program was "meant neither for skies nor earthly spot that did not exist, but for England." It was England of the Commonwealth, with Cromwell cast for the part of Lord Archon, "the sole legislator." His rule is tempered, however, by certain republican concessions to assure an advance over Stuart despotism. There is a ballot, "conveying this sap from the root, by an equal election or rotation, into the branches of magistracy or sovereign power." The most original feature is the agrarian law, "proportioned at two thousand pounds a year at such a balance that the power can never swerve out of the hands of the many." Taxes are assessed by group quota with excess or exemption based on the size of families. "If a man has ten children living, he shall pay no taxes; if he has five living, he shall pay but half taxes; if he has been married three years, or be above twenty-five years of age, and has no child or children lawfully begotten, he shall pay double taxes." Harrington's aristocratic creed leavened with a sense of justice is again expressed in his pithy distinction: "The wisdom of the few may be the light of mankind; but the interest of the few is not the profit of mankind."

In the early eighteenth century Simon Tyssot gives us the last theocracy in his deistic communism; while the African Mezzorania, discovered by the English Berington, and the South American Megapatagonia, discovered by the French Bretonne, are the last of the patriarchal Edens, with the usual stress on benevolent rulers and loyal subjects. Fontenelle's "Republic of Philosophers," on the Japanese archipelago Ajaonier, is governed by a Council of Twenty-four Elders, from fifty to sixty years of age.

Of the same general type is the Empire of Cantahar, projected by Varennes de Mondasse. On a bountiful plain three hundred leagues in diameter, encircled by snow-capped mountains, dwell a people all compact of temperance, sweetness, and wit, but swift to revenge. They enjoy the prestige and power insured by their strong army and navy. Among themselves virtue is rewarded so generously and vice punished so drastically that law-breaking is nobody's favorite pastime. After the age of fifteen every convicted criminal is doomed to chained servitude for life, with no hope of parole or pardon. Some are deported to the colonies and others kept as local public examples, for the salutary deterrent effect. This monarchy was established a thousand years ago by two hundred sages, from forty to sixty years of age, who decided on autocracy after a judicial weighing of all governmental forms. The ruler's title, Kincandior, signifies justice, clemency, and courage.

Another French Utopia of the eighteenth century, Mercier's Paris of the twenty-fifth century, is the first of the futurists and nearly a century ahead of the next one—a Dutch invention. But this new road to Utopia, blazed into the future instead of trailing back to the past or leading to a remote spot in the present, emerges into a terminal quite as quaint and conservative as any antique. For it too is a kingdom founded by a beneficent autocrat, where they still read by lamps and ride in carriages, and where nobody could think of a nicer reward for distinguished citizens than an embroidered hat presented by royalty's own hands. And as in Fénelon's *Telemachus,* there is a special training for the royal office, the dauphin being brought up as a commoner, ignorant of his high destiny while being put through the paces for it unaware. Public revenues are acquired by a universal five percent income tax, minus exemptions for the low-salaried, and plus the voluntary contributions of the wealthy and generous. These gifts are flung spontaneously and trustfully into large community chests standing open on the streets. Crime is, of course, nearly extinct, but the most vivid episode in the story is an account of a murderer's ceremonious execution.

Thus from the beginning down to the nineteenth century the favorite style in Utopian government is the aristocratic communism, and its little row of theocracies merely tightened the sanction by calling it divine. On the threshold of the new era stands appropriately the fairy isle Spensonia, where the single-tax idea first burgeons, where all land is leased for twenty-one years and then rerented at auction, where all share in the quarterly distribution of profits, where public affairs are managed by an Executive Council of twenty-four, and where illegitimate children are protected by law.

Not before this time even in Utopia was the aristocratic type of government questioned. And after democracy became an alternate it was far from setting the fashion. When Bulwer Lytton's haughty and exclusive Vrilya were defining democracy as Koom Posh, meaning Hollow Bosh, or the rule of the most debased and empty, they were on one side of the political fence. On the other side, to be sure, were spokesmen no less vehement and decisive. For by this Victorian Age the hitherto submerged nine-tenths had not only taken a prejudice against being submerged but had concluded it was foolish to lie prostrate just to be trampled on. They accordingly arose, with more vigor than grace, and began to take a hand in public polity, heedless of the shocked cries that they were also putting their foot in it. From then on, this acute partisanship is reflected in most of the Utopias, and with a more even division than might be supposed.

In view of the widespread and erroneous identification of Utopianism with Socialism, and of the increasing momentum of the whole democratic advance, it is particularly illuminating to observe that for the past century Utopian conservatism and radicalism stand at about half and half.

At the chronological head of this divergence New Holland offers an unintentional but fitting compromise. It is a federation in which all the land is owned by the central government as a unifying basis; aside from that, freedom is secured by allowing its eleven provinces to be kingdoms or republics at choice. Each citizen has from one to six property votes, and from one to three personal votes, the latter depending on his rating in an intelligence test. The highest scored are called Syndics and they alone qualify as jurors. As to penology, all prison sentences are indeterminate, and wages are paid for convict labor, so that a prisoner may work himself free.

Of a similar eclectic nature but in a more fantastic guise is Mantegazza's *L'Anno Tre Mille*, where the Islands of Experiments are leagued under the federal capital at Andropolis. Here the Pancrate devotes a month out of each year to sessions on international affairs. Among other things the State regulates birth and destroys inferior children. The separate districts cultivate their respective specialties by local option. In the Port of Equalization every citizen is dictator for one day, thus having a sip of pure authority. Terranopoli is a miniature Czarism of Church and State. Turano is ultra socialistic, featuring freedom in love and religion by acknowledging neither earthly nor heavenly father. Logopoli has an elected king and parliament. This versatile regime borders on such travesties as Moszkowski's *Isles of Wisdom* and Sweven's *Archipelago of Exiles*.

It has also a late, faint nineteenth century echo in *A Japanese Utopia* by Leonard Magnus. In the Land of Pe-Oh on the island of Atsa the shipwrecked Banosi finds himself in a highly cultured anarchy. Taxes are collected monthly in volunteered amounts, though by the advice of the leading business men. Punishment for any offense is by ostracism, a common Utopian discipline. Stubborn reactionaries are banished to Woo-dreda, as Sweven's recalcitrant Limanorans are to Riallero. The other islets pamper their own little specialties, such as the costuming for vocations on Ekadu.

No two Utopias could be more unlike than Fenimore Cooper's South Sea Crater and Ismar Thiusen's Nuiorc of the ninety-sixth century, yet they are two more variations of the republican model. The one is under the Colonial de luxe order of a gentleman governor for life supported by a cabinet of advisers. The other encourages private property but limits inheritance to twenty thousand dollars. The anonymous equatorial Colymbia is another aristocratic republic whose children are eugenically reared by the State.

Of all the republicans who are excessively anxious not to be identified with the socialists the most emphatic are a Frenchman and an Austrian. Thirion's Neustria, located in South America, is a counterblast to Cabet's Icaria, in North America, though the conservative constructionist admits he has no hope of rivalling the radical in popularity. His Utopian tale is a dramatization of his previous treatise on "Work, Liberty, and Property," and gives in full detail Neustria's Constitution. This platform is built of the usual planks: literate and property tests for voters, land highly taxed, employment guaranteed, insurance provided, money loaned at moderate interest to thrifty settlers, progress fostered by intra-district emulation.

Hertzka's Freeland, down in Africa, is a similar protest against the Bellamy type of communism. Its ardent proponent not only repudiates socialism and all its works but expressly disclaims being a Utopian. His own solution is indeed along the lines of cooperative industrialism but with the emphasis on free financial operations. Land is nationalized but all else is individualized. The President, instead of being Head of the Industrial Army, as in *Looking Backward*, is Head of the National Bank. Money is loaned without interest to promoters of new and worthy enterprises, but this public investment is safeguarded by the requirement of absolute publicity in the transactions. No fraudulent tricks can be played by the wily and unscrupulous under cover of secrecy.

The senatus-populique regime is emphasized by two more republics, Craig's Himalayan Ionia and Sweven's Antarctic Limanora. The Englishman's mountain colony relies mainly on its three laws: nationalization of land, restriction of inheritance, and race protection through applied eugenics. The Scotchman's island people pivot their ultra scientific and dynamic existence on the family. Here the household, always very small, is the focus of all activity, each one being assigned a research problem and held responsible for its solution. The temper of the place is strongly and scornfully anti-communistic. Gregariousness is ridiculed and discouraged because it thwarts personal development. Yet by nature and habit Limanoran life is transparent and unconcealed to a most unhuman extent.

Another government by the best, symbolized by its name, is Holford's Virginian Aristopia. It exhibits the familiar compromise of restricted inheritance and expanded suffrage. This principle is stretched to cover the rest of the United States by the administration of Colonel House's young reformer, Philip Dru. His new and improved Constitution, another one recorded at length, is still of the capitalistic and militaristic type, with such safety devices as the graded income tax, guaranteed employment, and the white light of publicity beating on the Wall Street throne. The presidential term is increased to ten years and the senatorial to life or good behavior, though the number of senators is reduced to one from each state.

Fairchild's City of Works is also avowedly anti-socialistic, yet it is a socialized municipality that provides telephones, transportation, and medical service. Business is carried on by trade guilds.

Frank Rosewater, who is almost as prolific of Utopias as H. G. Wells, pins his faith to one panacea which bobs up by various pseudonyms—Centrism, Proprietarism, Atlism. Whatever called, it is a scheme of double currency, designated as buy-money and sell-money. They operate by a system of forced reciprocal exchange which prevents hoarding, promotes circulation, keeps consumption at the same pace with production, and both going strong. Neither rent nor interest is allowed, nor yet any socialistic single-tax or profit-sharing.

Of such is the conservative line-up. But when we cross over to the opposition and mingle with these distrusted socialists, we find them quite as persuaded of the efficacy of their prescriptions as any of our doctrinaires.

Of importance as a pioneer is Edward Everett Hale, whose visit to the Italian Sybaris is recorded in a quietly persuasive manner. The Sybarite plan of loaning municipal umbrellas and collecting them after the rain anticipates Bellamy's great city umbrella of wide rubber awnings quickly adjusted over the streets, both symbolizing the manifest advantage of the whole cooperative regime. The Sybarite complete annotated inventory of all citizens is the germ of the universal registration and cataloguing in Wells's planetary Utopia. Our modern hectic sense of the value of time is gratified by the Sybaritic law that fines all late trains and people tardy at appointments, and requires a social caller to make a departing gesture every fifteen minutes—at the risk of having it accepted. The hand of authority is also felt in larger matters. Youths must marry or be exiled. On the other hand, old age pensions are provided, though only for bare subsistence. Suffrage is granted to all men and women who register. Registration is voluntary but carries with it liability to military service, ladies being placed in the artillery.

Aside from the many minor echoes and imitations, two French socialistic pictures are drawn in Anatole France's *White Stone* (last chapter) and in Émile Zola's *Work;* two English in Morris's *News from Nowhere* and Blatchford's *Sorcery Shop;* and two American in Howells's *The Eye of the Needle* and Bellamy's *Looking Backward,* this last continued in sequels by himself and others.

Edward Bellamy is of course the Big Chief among Utopian socialists, and is dedicated to the industrial-economic settlement of the political problem. His prophetic soul sees in the year 2000 the entire population of this country enrolled in the vast Labor Army whose Generalissimo is President of the United States. His Cabinet is composed of the Heads of the various Guilds, and his Congress meets only at the end of the five-year presidential term. The government is entirely in the hands of the emeriti, retired at forty-five from active occupation, and these are invested with an authority a feudal baron would have envied. Workers are not even allowed to vote, and have only a still small voice in running their own affairs. But since their affairs are so admirably run by those elders to whose status all are only too rapidly approaching, they have little use for any voice at all.

Although centralized in Boston, Bellamy's plan operates throughout the United States, forming the largest Utopian territory up to that date. Fifteen years later the United States of Europe are presented by William Stanley as a federation accomplished half a century sooner, in 1950. As revealed by the hypnotized poet, Theodore Fox, a congress of delegates met in 1934 and decided on this political union. At the first regular meeting of the representatives Paris was chosen as the European capital, with English as the official language (phonetically spelled) and a German elected as President of the Superior Legislative Assembly. This body, known as the States' House of Lords, numbers nearly a thousand members, each one standing for half a million constituents. They are elected every three years by postal-ballot, and are organized into twenty committees of fifty each. These groups deal with such matters as religion, medicine, science and art, as well as more political items. Special training in the field concerned is a prerequisite for membership, and at that a new member does not vote for the first year. A capitalist must also have an academic Ph.D. to insure breadth of interests. Three members from each committee combine into a Central Council of sixty. The President is elected by this International

Parliament, and is up for reelection every year. Naturally, only international affairs are handled by this Assembly, which holds two sessions annually, of three months each. The different countries continue with their local governments.

In Great Britain, for instance, the four hundred members of the House of Commons are elected by initiative vote, and the three hundred of the Senate (substituted for the old House of Lords) either promoted from the Commons or appointed by the President; this to fill vacancies caused by death. The former Prince of Wales is now the elected President. Women have the suffrage and are eligible to all offices except the States' House of Lords. In most of the states revenue comes from a graded income tax, with exemptions for small salaries, dependents, misfortunes, and so on. An Idlers' Tax of two percent is levied on all the able-bodied under fifty-five who cannot produce a gainful occupation. Taxes are no longer needed for military purposes, as peace is an accomplished fact. Law has become identified with justice, crime is diagnosed as mental aberration and corrected by isolation, and capital punishment abolished.

The other continents are similarly organized, North America now including Canada and Mexico. Mr. Stanley crowds Mr. Wells somewhat in the cosmic scope, besides beating him to it by two years.

The total effect of this survey is the impression

that even the thoroughly democratized modern Ship of State continues to list heavily to starboard. Captains and officers may be elected by an ever widening suffrage instead of by their fortunate stars, but they sit just as firmly in command. Their tenure is held, however, with this difference, that their interference and regulation is no longer for the benefit of the boss but of the subordinate; and the latter is really a coordinate in the ultimate diffusion of authority that neutralizes any temporary inequality. And if the citizen is deprived of his inalienable right to loaf, shirk, and be a parasite, he is by way of compensation assured of a decent job, a living wage, and a comfortable old age. His liberty may be curtailed but his life is protected and his pursuit of happiness is less of an obstacle race. And as long as freedom and even justice are secondary to safety and good management, the mass of humanity, devoid of skill and power, incapable of little but stewing in its own juice and weltering in its own disorder, may well be cheerfully content with its enforced welfare.

While Utopia at large is not unified enough to agree on a single theory or consistent practice of government, its general tendency is strikingly symbolized by its official architecture, both by the elimination of certain familiar buildings and by the introduction of strange new ones.

Most conspicuous by their absence or rarity are

law courts, jails, reformatories and prisons. Utopia accords small space to cell or cloister. This unanimous pushing of the whole legal apparatus off the boards comes from practising the simple precept that a gram of prevention is worth several tons of cure, and that it is the function of the State to be beforehand with the prevention instead of behindhand with the cure. Much is made also of the lack of criminal incentive in a land of fair opportunity where a normally inoffensive citizen is not goaded to law-breaking by the maddening unreasonableness of that law.

One looks in vain likewise for poor-houses, insane asylums, sweat-shops, slums, and their concomitant opposites, jewelry stores and palatial hotels. Hotels of any kind are scarce, for that matter, their place being supplied by the public guest-houses which are more like an extension of the home. From the capacious Strangers' House in Bacon's Bensalem to the similar institutions in Wells's World State, this provision for civic hospitality is a point of pride. It graces Ajaonier, New Britain, Altruria, and Kalomera; also Donnelly's African elysium, Benson's future London, and Thiusen's future New York.

Another structure in the more recent Utopias presents a queer paradox. This is the Hall of Euthanasia, vestibule to facile death. It serves three purposes—for suicide, for executions, and for the kind putting away of the unfortunate who, though neither criminals nor sinners, are yet unfitted to live. Alike for the sufferers from hypochondria who crave release for their own sakes, for the incorrigibles who must be released for society's sake, and for the deficient or incurable doomed to a vegetative or agonized existence, the lethal chamber is regarded as the most merciful way out.

Of all these the most elaborately beautiful and eloquently portrayed is in Jaeger's *The Question Mark*. A gleaming white marble palace adorns its magnificent gardens, kept in perpetual bloom by underground heating, made entrancing by perfumed fountains and crystal lakes. You may wander through this colorful and musical fairyland, you may enter the spacious interior lined with alcoves each furnished with a luxuriously cushioned divan. You almost succumb to the aramanthol-charged air and the cadence of the haunting lotus song. It is by an imperceptible, wellnigh irresistible, movement that you relax on one of those inviting couches; and by so doing you automatically release the gentle but fatal current that lulls into dreamless eternal sleep.

Utopian government may then assume jurisdiction over all life. It may decide whether you shall be born, how long you shall live, when and how you shall be educated, how hard you shall work and for what wages, wherewithal you shall be clothed, and what kind of a funeral you shall have. It may invade your home, abduct your children, and herd you into the municipal hall for dinner. It may impose both death and taxes. Nevertheless, as it evolves more and more from the prohibitive stage with its galling shackles and bars, to the beneficent constructive power that carries on enterprises too large and complicated for individual management, its dignity and utility quite offset its usurpation of personal privileges, and evoke loyal pride and fervent patriotism. And if this powerful institution cannot guarantee to all its citizens a life successful enough to be worth living, it can at least make death worth dying, and rob the grave of its sting.

Altogether, whatever chimerical aspect Utopian government may have, it does not lie in its own nature, for that, even at its most radical, is quite conventional and centralized and laudably respectable. It is no paradise for anarchists. Though the judicial branch is nearly atrophied from disuse, the legislative is in vigorous condition, and the executive rejoices as the strong man to run his race.

Where it is deluded is in its sanguine confidence in human nature, viewing it as sagacious and altruistic when ruling, tractable and competent when ruled. But it is precisely his confidence that what is not yet may sometime be that encourages the Utopian in his sturdy hope. He unrolls this hope with a touching belief that if the world once could be made to see what a good government would be like if it could be got, it would be at more pains to get it.

CHAPTER III

EDUCATION

If education were merely the "leading out" implied by its etymology, it would be a short process and soon over. But since nothing can be brought out of anything that has not first been put in by some means or other, that is only the second half of it. What goes into a living organism becomes so transformed by the miracle known as metabolism that it comes out as a new and original creation. This constant reciprocal action results in the growth that marks every thing alive from birth to senility.

Education is directed growth; hence the giving out will not be exhausted as long as the taking in continues. The complementary rhythm of life includes, along with labor and rest, craving and appeasement, pleasure and pain, this absorption of raw material and exporting of recreated products. Knowledge, whether first hand experience or second hand information, is the grist out of which wisdom is manufactured.

Nature herself sees to this growth and manufacture, but she is too unconcerned with symmetry

EDUCATION

and economy, too fond of the grotesque and vagrant, too careless with the noxious and deadly, fully to be trusted. The human gardener has to step in with his selected seeds, sprinkler, shears and what-not to insure cultivated products. With human plants the need for this direction is the more urgent because they are not static and passive. They have to act as well as exist and must be equipped for sustained and arduous effort. This developing business brings into play the shrewdest science and the finest art.

Since Utopia is a symbol of the higher civilization, it might be expected to specialize on education. For if this directed growth is a preparation for life, it would seem the more valuable the life the more momentous the preparation. But such is not the case. It will not take us very long to make the rounds of Utopia's schools and colleges. We shall be let out early, not because we are hurrying through in the perfunctory visiting manner, but because the Utopians themselves have been rather perfunctory in this department.

That these world-makers should be less preoccupied with education than with government is, however, explicable enough. In the first place, the actual discussion of a point is not always in direct ratio to its importance. Sometimes the most vital things are taken for granted. In the second place, schoolcraft is as technical as statecraft. Utopians are usually laymen in both fields. A few delight in constructing constitutions and mapping out curricula. But the majority are content to dismiss these details with honorable mention. And such specifications being omitted from formal learning, not so much is left.

This explains why only about a third of the Utopians mention education at all, and why only half that number describe it beyond the elementary stage. The Greek pioneers did indeed stress heavily the nurture of youth and were interested in ways and means, but they conceived the school as a mill meant to grind out good and efficient fodder for the State. The Persian method was concentrated on producing capable rulers. Spartan lads were encouraged to steal as useful practice for future soldiers plundering from the enemy. Athenian boys were brought up on literature carefully expurgated and music strictly censored in the interests of morality, the moral being the expedient and instrumental for citizenship. Athenian girls had the same discipline, especially in gymnastics, to fit them for motherhood, though their children were not to be theirs to have and to hold or even to be told apart from others in the common nursery.

Socrates waxes eloquent on the theme: "Like those who take colts amid noise and tumult to see if they are of a timid nature, so we must take our youth amid terrors of some kind, and again pass them into pleasures, and prove them more thoroughly than gold is proved in the furnace, that we may discover whether they are armed against all enchantments, and of a noble bearing always."

Those who pass this test are to become the Guardians, for they have taken "the dye of the laws in perfection." Over the Third Estate, however, no such vigilance is necessary. "Education," continues the sage, "is a thing which I would rather call not great but sufficient for our purpose," since "if our citizens are well educated, and grow into sensible men, they will easily see their way through all these, as well as other matters which I omit."

Centuries later, Raphael Hythloday describes his unique discovery under eight several topics, but education is not one of them. He dismisses that subject in a parenthetical remark under the heading of religion; saying that "the education of youth belongs to the priests, yet they do not take so much care of instructing them in letters as in forming their minds and manners aright; they use all possible methods to infuse very early into the tender and flexible minds of children such opinions as are both good in themselves and will be useful to their country." This does not mean that the intellect is neglected. The people are naturally studious. They arise at unholy hours to attend instructive lectures, convert their meal times into sessions of mental improvement, and spend their leisure moments in reading. They seize promptly on the imported invention of printing and perfect it. They allow the few who show real interest in advanced learning to devote their lives to it, released from other toil. And as for scientific appliances, incubator-chickens in the early sixteenth century were something of a novelty.

Johann Andreae had far more enthusiasm for the cause than did Thomas More. His Christianopolis is provided with dormitories for the very young, with an alternate program whereby the boys study in the mornings and play in the afternoons, and the girls reverse the order. Much care is devoted to manual and vocational training. Older students are instructed in the history and principles of their trades and occupations in order to make the mastery of them more intelligent and therefore more interesting. Great pride is taken in this new inductive method that has replaced the old "stuffing of inexperience." The crown of the whole system, dominant building and citadel, "innermost shrine and center of activity," is the college. Its twelve halls, occupying four floors, house the library, art gallery, laboratories, archives, printing press, and armory, though they trust the last will always stand idle. The curriculum of eight departments furnishes a wide range of instruction. Next to this source of mental illumination, the greatest pride is in the literal nightlights of the city, for they symbolize Andreae's ideal that man should "turn more to the light!" Even the Sun City has less radiance.

It has, however, quite as much zeal for learning, and the same view of it as a joyful experience. Campanella's special contribution is the germ of our moving pictures, only there it is the students who do the moving. The circular city has a series of seven concentric walls forming backs and fronts of the solid and continuous buildings. Both the convex and concave sides of these curving structures are "adorned with the finest pictures." Around this pictorial panorama circulates the peripatetic school, conning the rhymed explanations. In attendance are "magistrates who announce the meaning of the pictures, and boys are accustomed to learn all the sciences, without toil and as if for pleasure." This inclusive scope is not greatly exaggerated as "all," for the illustrations include botany, zoology, entomology, ornithology, ichthyology, geography, geology, astronomy, mathematics, chemistry, medicine, biography, history, sociology, and technology. Aside from this, the children are given much educative play, with considerable military practice. Adults continue their abstruse as well as practical studies, and hold their scholars most noble and renowned. Teachers and professors are "men approved before all others," and are influential in the government. Among the learned doctors are Astrologus, Cosmographus, Rhetor, Medicus, and Moralis. They all teach from one huge volume, a sort of scientific bible. The Chief Executive, Hoh (Metaphysics), "is ashamed to be ignorant of any possible thing." These knowledge lovers anticipated the Bensalemites and the New Britainers in sending out "explorers and ambassadors over the whole earth, who learn thoroughly the customs, forces, rule and history of the nations, bad and good alike."

It is this Bensalem of Bacon's that is the very temple of scholarship and erudition but it has little traffic with popular education. Its aim is to collect rather than scatter information. Its "Merchants of Light," travelling incognito over the world, are investigating squads sent to scout around and bring back reports how to do. Saloman's House is a vast research laboratory buzzing with experimental industry. Specialists go about in neat little triads, the Mystery Men, the Dowry Men, the Lamps, the Inoculators, the Interpreters. There are deep caves for refrigeration, high towers for meteorology, artificial minerals and pre-Burbank hybrids. And nothing in the whole story is told with more éclat than the incident of a sumptuous pageant showing how to treat a Major Professor.

Again in the Kingdom of Ophir is reflected the Teutonic love of the university and care for the intellect. Illiteracy is unknown, teachers skilled and superior, and a Council of Education meets weekly

EDUCATION

to contemplate projects for improvement. A Professor of Economy is installed because "it is considered very disadvantageous and unsuitable for a learned man who understands all other sciences not to be familiar with domestic economics, and often to be surpassed therein by the most insignificant persons."

Ophir is located in Palestine, along with Samuel Gott's Solyma, and this "Jerusalem Regained" is in its different way almost as much of a specialized educational Utopia as New Atlantis, and as Spartan in its discipline as the rule of Lycurgus. Youth immured in barracks, gates guarded by stern porters, early rising, frugal eating, uniform dressing, and seven years between visits home, all this has little Utopian savor. But if herein the Puritan Gott faces backward, as does the Lutheran Andreae in his approval of fasting and whipping for stupid or stubborn children, he faces forward in his scholarships for the poor, his technical schools and workshops for the masses, his University Extension in the form of "public discourses held frequently in all parts of the land, not only of a religious nature, but on ethics, the family life, and such topics." These, however, are served sparingly to commoners, on the apprehension that, although as much learning should be given as can be assimilated, too much culture induces discontent.

Nor does the nineteenth century inaugurate what

might be called a sweeping change. The Victorian Britishers have no brief for mass education. Morris tosses it off with the concession that "most children, seeing books lying about, manage to read by the time they are four years old." But if they do not, Morris thinks it is no great matter. What is there worth reading? Our contemporary American who declares that "history is bunk" has at least one English and one French Utopian as precedent. And if one should have a taste for languages Morris supposes he could pick up half a dozen with his left hand.

Lytton's Coming Race are an exceedingly intelligent people and well aware that science is power. But they can dispense with the grammar grades, since their ten-year-old is the mental age of the adult visitor from earth's upper crust. And they are rather dubious about intellectual pursuits, esteeming them a harmless pastime for the ladies. The charming and accomplished Zee is a professor in the College of Sages and happily devoted to her "unpractical studies." More practical is the general utilizing of the subconscious mind. It is a great convenience, for example, to educate the ignorant English intruder while he sleeps—a device employed also by the Limanorans, another race to specialize in science.

Robert Pemberton, however, reverts to the earlier emphasis. In his Happy Colony the ten colleges form the centers of the ten circular cities. The entire school period is sliced into three divisions of seven years each. The first is a herald of the modern nursery-schools for pre-school age. Babes accompanied by their mothers congregate in the Infant Temple and Theater, open during a twelve-hour day, from six to six. The two main subjects are music and manners. As soon as they can understand simple talk these tiny tots attend fifteen minute lectures which deal out information in a practical and illustrated way concerning the vocabulary and tools of daily living. Everything is dramatized but no time is wasted on baby-talk, toy-rubbish, or futile discipline. Gymnastics merge into work-play. Languages are featured for the sake of international-mindedness. Throughout the next two periods this primary instruction and method develops into vocational training and intellectual culture. In the third stage, from the ages of fourteen to twenty-one, all students work half of each day and study the other half, boys and girls alternating as in Christianopolis.

William Stanley agrees on the wisdom of beginning early to teach the child about the world of his daily life and operations. But in his zeal for the polytechnic school, mechanics, and applied science, he does not neglect the values of applied art. In 1950 homes are beautified by the hand-made treasures the children bring from their creative schools.

The two Frenchmen who also dream of a future Paris have definite if incomplete ideas on this subject. Louis Mercier would abolish the classics to make room for more modern studies, and sponsors the first educational theater. Anatole France would substitute music and art for law and theology, and exhibits his communism fostering the higher learning, for utilitarian purposes if no others. "Study, just as much as work," he says, "entitles one to existence." Another Frenchman, Émile Thirion, endows his Patagonian Neustria with several state colleges and a university that grants only the doctor's degree.

The Russian Merejkowski follows the English Morris in keeping the Tree of Knowledge out of his Garden of Eden and thus cheating the serpent out of his vantage point for temptation. His Earthly Paradise is bovinely idyllic. Its contented cherubim are by choice unschooled and illiterate because they believe that ignorance truly is bliss, that all this traffic with books is a laborious and exacting futility, not worth its pains and sacrifice, and leading only to discouragement and wretchedness. The visitor is told how in the old days learning and publication multiplied until in the twenty-fifth century the race was swamped in its own print and obliged in self-defense to abolish the nuisance. They did this with the same righteous satisfaction with which Mercier's Parisians made a mighty bonfire of useless or pernicious books. One episode in Merejkowski's tale concerns a lad found weeping bitterly by himself. On being questioned he admitted he had been aroused and inspired by the stranger's account of the knowledge and mentality in his own country, and had become ashamed of his benighted state, convicted of the sin of ignorance. The boy's misery is promptly assuaged by the promise of having his wish to study granted, and he is indeed packed right off to school. The patriarch Jesrar then explains that he had at once recognized this morbid desire for learning as a case of atavism, inherent no doubt but precipitated by this particular circumstance. The school to which the youth was sent was really an asylum. Over on another island they kept an educational institution for the care and possible cure of just such patients. At present it had about three hundred inmates.

The three or four Americans interested in the subject show a similar variety. Cooper's only concern with education is to furnish grade schools on his Crater where the children are taught "only what they ought to learn," and that is not much. The schooling of Hale's Sybarite youngsters is restricted in quantity but of good quality. The year is so quartered that pupils attend three winter and three summer months, four hours a day, with a teacher for every twenty students. The other six months are spent in recreation and practice-work in trades, the order of attendance being rotated from year to year. (A scrap called *The Milltillionaire* advocates a like scheme wherein two school terms of four months apiece alternate with two vacations of two months, the latter partly employed in vocational practice.) To discourage pedagogical graft, no Sybarite professor is allowed to teach from his own text unless it is recommended by the Council of Education. And to encourage general reading, the Public Library is open day and night, so that if a sleepless citizen should feel like hobnobbing with books at three A.M. he has that privilege. The tradition is that the building never has been closed since Herodotus read and wrote there.

In the Nuiorc of Thiusen's Diothas all bridal couples are required to spend in college the six months following the honeymoon, the husband studying law, and the wife taking courses in medicine, nursing, and household economics. Much more thorough is Bellamy's future Boston, for everyone graduates from the public college, its diploma appropriately celebrating youth's coming of age and joining the Industrial Army. Schindler's sequel to this story portrays "Young West," son of Julian and Edith, progressing happily from the nursery school to his bachelor's degree.

These instances may suffice to indicate how little Utopia has to offer that is novel or original in education. Such prediction as there is lies mainly in the early schemes wherein the School is fostered by the State, one being as orthodox as the other. This was something of an innovation in the days when the State and Church alliance was accepted as the true and natural combination, when Church and School were identified, but when State and School were not regarded as suitable partners. When a man's belief was reckoned more important than his knowledge, religion was logically a public charge and education a private. When his creed became his personal affair and his enlightenment a social concern and responsibility, the situation was reversed accordingly. Whereas society used to be anxious about your soul and inquired how pure was your heart, it now is troubled about your mind and asks how high is your I.Q.

In this shifting of values Utopia takes its educational cue from reality rather than doing it the other way around. But if it is satisfied with its provision for complete juvenile schooling and incomplete culture on the ground that the higher learning is a more or less optional and negligible luxury, Utopia is at least consistent. It regards education as primarily vocational and secondarily cultural, and lets it go at that. One must be taught how to work efficiently. To play delightfully and to enrich and grace one's whole personality are also matters of great importance, but they can be left to personal adjustment. Released and well provisioned individuals may be trusted to get these things for themselves.

The Utopian may well adopt as his slogan the exhortation—

"Up! up! my Friend, and quit your books"— for it takes plenty of holidays to make a paradise. The truly perfected life would have no more use for slates and desks and blackboards than heaven has need of plows and washtubs. These discounts on bliss are admitted in most Utopias, not exactly as evils, but as necessary compromises in any existence, however ideal, that is still to remain human. Education is considered at best a means to an end rather than an end in itself.

CHAPTER IV

OCCUPATION

Work is cut off the same paradox as society and jurisdiction. We hate it and we hate the lack of it. The Utopian problem is to make two hates equal one love. For if government is the backbone of civilization, labor is its sinew and muscle. One is as necessary as the other to any life above the jelly-fish stage. Accordingly, what cannot be rejected must be accepted. But in an idealistic station acceptances are always "with pleasure," never marred by sullen reluctance or suppressed defiance.

Utopians have recognized the fundamental nature of both government and labor by making them equally pervasive and prominent in their schemes. They are, however, more unanimous in their opinion about how to work (or to be worked) than how to be ruled. There is no distinct line of cleavage, as between radical and conservative, and such difference as there is comes largely from the political opposition,—whether or not labor shall be under governmental direction.

Most of these State Makers have discovered that all work is divided into three parts: routine drudgery, professional employment, and creative activity. The first of these is the largest and most barren territory, and it is this desert that must be made to blossom as the rose. The Utopian might accomplish this transformation by waving a magic wand, but to his credit be it said that this is not his favorite method. Only in the chronological extremes is excessive leisure possible. The balmy and bounteous Terrae Australes of earlier date are indolent Elysiums where there is literally nothing doing. Unclothed and unhoused you may lie on the flowerbed and let ripe fruit drop into your mouth. In the later scientific Paradises everything is done by machinery. Daintily costumed and amid elegant surroundings you press a button. You do not even have to await results. They are instantaneous.

But between these golden extremes of nature's plenty and man's ingenuity stretches the leaden mean. Yet this, dull and heavy as it is, may be lightened and brightened to an incredible extent. The lightening is secured by objective manipulation. The total amount of toil is reduced by eliminating the superfluous; and the proportionate amount is diminished by an equitable distribution. Adequate payment is guaranteed. The brightening is achieved by inducing the ready and willing mood which comes partly from a satisfied sense of justice and partly from bringing into play the active side of human psychology, the subjective solution.

The first policy sounds so absurdly simple as to be axiomatic. A child could figure out that if everybody worked, including father—and mother—nobody would be having too much of a bad thing, so far as it is bad. And a moron should be able to see the folly of making a lot of things that do nobody any good, and a lot more that do positive harm to all who purchase and partake. It is putting the principles of these admitted facts into practice that challenges the Utopian. The second policy is more complex and ramifies into other departments, but it rests on the simple circumstance of having time and energy to be disposed of.

In the matter of getting the hard, repellent, and monotonous drudgery done, Utopias reflect the development of real life. Not only the old Greek regime but the other side of the Medieval span rested frankly on the institution of slavery. Plato barely mentions slaves in passing, but even the free artisans of his Republic are to have no leisure for poor health or any such luxury. When a carpenter falls ill, for instance, he takes some rough and ready cure, whereupon he "either gets well and lives and does his business or dies and has no more trouble."

Centuries later Thomas More did not scruple to have the disagreeable jobs turned off by slaves and war-captives. In the fantastic World of Mercury the lazy and stubborn were punished by servitude; the comparatively recent Oriental Ajaomei used slave labor; and Merejkowski's twenty-seventh century Paradise is maintained by domesticated subhumans who are quite content to perform the simple services required, with comfortable homes and kind treatment as payment. In Paul Adam's Borneo they consider criminals the proper stuff to make soldiers out of, and their army is composed of vicious but desexed men and women.

In the main, however, Utopia transfers the compulsion from outer to inner pressure by the processes already mentioned. The curtailed working day runs a gamut of from three to eight hours. About four hours is the allotment in Christianopolis, and this precedent is followed in Megapatagonia, where the working age is from twenty to a hundred and fifty; in Intermere, where they have a five-day week; and in Altruria, where a quaint regulation asks all newly-weds to perform one day's labor together before starting on their honeymoon, in order to demonstrate the dignity and pleasure of work.

The duty is raised to five or six hours a day in the Crescent Island and in Calejava; likewise in Freeland, where all able-bodied men under sixty carry on their voluntary cooperative guilds (the guild system is also featured by Harrington, Morris, and others), having been trained for their professions with the zeal of the Christianopolites; in Icaria, where the working age is from eighteen to sixty-five; in Ionia, where the populace breakfasts at eight, works from nine to three, dines at four, and plays the rest of the day; in Kalomera, where they are relieved by the seasonal transfers inaugurated by More, and released at the age of fifty-five; in Stanley's United States of Europe, where too they retire at fifty-five, after a labor schedule of a five-hour day and a five-day week, on an annual average, with flexible margins for seasonal industries; on Simpson's Mars, and in the Dream City of Unitas; in Vetsch's Sonnenstadt, where the work-year is 260 days and the retiring age is fifty; and in Salisbury's future New York, where any citizen not caring to put in the required four to six hours per day for two hundred days a year is free to labor or to loaf on any unreclaimed spot he can find.

The eight-hour day is rare, but it occurs among the South Sea Sevarites and in the French Socialism of Petaud and Pouget. Lytton's Vrilya have a twenty-hour day, divided into eight Silent, eight Earnest, and four Easy Hours, although the hardest is easy enough.

The matter of remuneration joins labor to economics and ties it up with government. Under any kind of capitalistic system it is catch as catch can, though in Utopia the catching is so good that there is plenty for all. Under any kind of socialized cooperation the State is the paymaster, assumes all living expenses, and provides such extras as trans portation, entertainment, education, medical service, in short, the conventional necessities and all the luxuries the law allows.

Apparently by common consent Utopians conscript their children and youths for this routine labor. The Diothas get their drudgery done by the Zerdars and Zeruans, lads and maidens from seventeen to twenty-five, but they are on salary and spice the work with periods of play and foreign travel. This plan anticipates Bellamy's more elaborate program, whereby the Subpoenaed Sons and Daughters of the State are drafted into the Industrial Army upon graduation from college. The uniform wage for all citizens is two thousand dollars a year (not so small from the 1887 point of view) and the variation is made in amount of time. The harder and more repugnant the toil the less of it required, down to one hour a day if necessary.

The salary is issued in the form of annual nontransferable coupon-books and these coupons may be spent entirely according to the owner's taste and preference. In his *Birth of Freedom* H. B. Salisbury adopts the same plan for his socialistic New York as Bellamy's for Boston, with the added convenience that the ticket-books contain small change down to minutes and seconds, for use in the slot-machines where one gets his daily paper and such trifles. A view is given of a charmingly appointed factory where beautiful girls work for four hours a day. Since one work-hour will pay for a whole day's living in the most sumptuous hotel (at that time the Grand Central Station on Staten Island) there can be no question of making both ends meet on the ordinary scale of maintenance.

Alfred Ollivant also borrows from Bellamy, especially featuring the Industrial Army idea. His story *Tomorrow* opens with a picture of the elaborate ceremony of the Service Year celebration. All youths of eighteen are mustered in and placed in individual homes assigned by a committee and always in some district far from their own homes. Here they remain for ten years, disciplined by their foster-parents into a sweet subdued humility. Labor is mainly hand-craft and agricultural, for all live the simple life in Garden Hamlets, as this part of their gospel is according to Morris. The eleventh year is devoted to a sabbatical holiday and the choosing of a permanent occupation. The choice is free but must be ratified by the supervising Council. The emergence from probation is not, however, automatic, for if any unfortunate twenty-eight-year-old has not earned his Certificate of Freedom he is classed with the Drops and Lags, and compelled to serve two days for every day lost. No excuse is granted for illness, because sane people do not allow themselves to become sick. The fortunate graduates who are not flunked out for laziness or disobedience are then divided into two classes called

Contents or Aspirants, according as their ambitions are static or dynamic; that is, whether they are satisfied with a passing grade in the School of Life or want to go out for Honors.

Hellenbach's island of Mellonta is another Eden where the work is done mainly by children. From five to fifteen they are domestic helpers. From fifteen to eighteen the boys do the general catering and provisioning; from eighteen to thirty they are field-workers and craftsmen; from thirty to forty-five they do odd jobs more or less at their own option; and from forty-five to sixty they act as patriarchal governors, like Bellamy's rule of the emeriti. Meanwhile the girls are Vestals from fifteen to twenty-two, and Mothers until they are retired. The visiting stranger is given his choice of cultivating flowers or fruit and chooses fruit. He also goes with the crowd on a sample labor expedition. Fifty men and fifty maids, all dressed picturesquely for the part, walk to the woods, where they toil for four hours cutting and clearing and incidentally getting a tremendous appetite for the gay picnic dinner. Then they all frolic along home during the afternoon.

This idyllic agriculture follows the precedent of Campanella, whose Sun City residents march to the country in seedtime and harvest led by flags, drums and trumpets. The seasonal shift from town to country is provided also by More, Morris, Ellis, Howells, and others, who have the whole population swinging back and forth from urban to rural life. A more modern method, used by Rosewater, Rossi, Saunders, and others, is to have the farmers live in town and commute to their fields, a transit made easy by automobiles.

Believing in the slogan that change of occupation is rest, the Utopians make considerable effort to secure the change. Much more important than the seasonal transfer, which is largely for public convenience, is the avocation, which contributes to personal pleasure. Nothing in Utopia is exhibited with more pride and delight than this bioccupational scheme. William Morris revels in the idea of his boatman working in metals, the weaver being a mathematician, the dustman writing reactionary novels. Anatole France introduces his Michael, baker and statistician. Ismar Thiusen is complacent over Ialma doing hosiery and art photography, Ulmene weaving cloth and composing music, Utis being a physician and maker of bolts and microscopes. It is Robert Blatchford who out-Herods them all. His Mr. Lascelles of the Sorcery Shop does, to be sure, stop with merely mending lightning-rods and writing novels; and Dorothy Suthers is content to make rugs and sing in opera. But Elizabeth Groom must be a coppersmith and multilinguist; Mr. Norris can handle his astronomy and specialize in roses, mosaics and tapestries; and Hilda Parker is versatile enough to be a librarian, maker of musical instruments, landscape painter, and authority on natural history. After this, Alfred Ollivant is a mild disciple, saving his creative diversions for the solace of old age. His Flam is a blacksmith and Professor of the Clothes Epoch in History, but Master Anthony is a carpenter for fun and fascinated by his experiments in "antique" carriages; and Mistress Miriam is happy in weaving a blue silk gown for her ward Mary's graduation.

That these congenial avocations may be described either as work or play indicates that this is just another of life's little subtleties. It is not so inconsistent as it sounds to say that our ardent longing to do something is equalled only by our ardent longing to do nothing. These contrary states are not synchronous. To do what we like when we like would indeed be ideal, and by the same token anarchical. To conquer anarchy even Utopia stoops to compromises.

For the Utopians are at least smart enough to appreciate our mortal predicament of having to put in our time. "How to live on twenty-four hours a day" is only half the problem. The other half is living the twenty-four hours, multiplied by thousands of days. To accomplish this without falling into vacuous vegetating or aimless frittering or expensive folly, not to mention degenerating into vice and crime, is the noblest of all Utopian ambitions.

The shrewder of them further discern that using up our time is only half the demand. The other half is using up ourselves. Only from an overworked and enslaved people could have come the legend of labor being a curse for disobedience. Such would naturally look back on the Garden of Eden and forward to the orthodox Heaven as Paradises of Nothing to Do. The Utopian Paradise is a place where everybody has enough business to keep from being bored and nobody has enough to hound him into nervous prostration.

It would seem no more than reasonable that all souls should feel in the pink of condition and in hearty accord with the doctrine that it is right for man to "rejoice in his works and enjoy good in all his labor," yet it is precisely here that the Utopians are most obliged to sentimentalize in order to accredit their optimism. Time and again we are given an exhibition of how the Won't Work is converted into the Must Work, by drastic methods if external compulsion has to be used. Morelly, for instance, is sure that life according to the Code de la Nature will be one long frolicking picnic with just enough hay-making and butter-churning to give it a fillip, yet somehow the watchful eye of an elderly director is needed over small groups of from five to twenty.

It is the Altruria of Dean Howells that furnishes the most amusing display of unconscious inconsistency. These people lead an incomparable life with only three hours a day of Obligatories, the remaining twenty-one being Voluntaries. One day a private yacht is wrecked on their halcyon shores and its passengers indefinitely marooned. When their store of supplies is exhausted these involuntary guests are forced by their kindly hosts to work or starve, because such is the custom of the country and it is a country where neither English titles nor American dollars can buy a bite to eat. After some argument the gentlefolk yield more or less gracefully, and refractory members of the crew are brought to diligence by mild shocks from electrified steel nets in which they are enclosed. The reason given for this insistence that the strangers at least do light housekeeping or landscape gardening is that the spectacle of their idle and pampered luxury would demoralize the natives. Under this pernicious influence they would doubtless strike for a two-hour day and demand the dazzling gold and silver coins to play with.

On the whole, however, there is nothing ridiculous in the Utopian Will to Work. Andreae's Christianopolites, who "never approached a piece of work without alacrity" because they were "not driven like pack animals," set a good Utopian pace. And if they could also "climb to the lofty citadel of virtue over the difficult hills of work," they literally made a virtue out of necessity, as well as pleasure out of both. As long as pleasure throws her whole weight into the play side of the scale, work naturally kicks the beam. When she puts one foot over into the work side, she does something toward equalizing the balance. The early primitive Utopians had to effect this alliance between work and pleasure by simplified living and mental attitude. The later modernized ones are able to invoke the magician Applied Science.

The power-rods of Lytton's Vrilya make routine work so easy it is all done by children. The power-boxes of Jaeger's future Londoners give their owners immediate command over heat, light, motion, and all such essentials. The Intermerans tap their electricity directly from the air, and use it to pulverize rock, propel their medocars and merocars and aerocars, cook their food and refrigerate it, and print bulletins in ten minutes. The Kalomerans, who run about in their poised gyroscopic cars, send their fiber and paper clothing back to the pulp factory after one wearing, as they do on Wells's planet and other places. Whole cities are built of malleable and unbreakable glass, notably the ualin of the Diothas.

This method of solving the employment problem might lead to the reverse problem of unemployment were it not counteracted by the social guarantee against poverty, since people are not afraid of being idle so much as of being poor. The Utopian philosophy of labor is not wholly impracticable once their premise is granted of a population healthy, happy, intelligent and prosperous. Such a people can lick their tasks and chores into shape between any two meals, and have the rest of the time for fun.

Fun may involve more arduous toil than any drudgery, but for all that, it belongs to another department of living—the felicitous spending of leisure time.

CHAPTER V

RECREATION

It is the play side of life that is identified with the pleasure side. And that is what makes it important. Cheerful as we may be over our work, it is in our amusement that we wax merry and glad. Indeed it is the prospect of that reward that induces resignation to otherwise insulting toil. In the workaday world where drudgery is incessant the annual holiday is anticipated with relish the long year through, and when so soon over, prolonged by joyful reminiscence.

Utopia's leading ambition is to inscribe at the end of every day—

A Good Time Was Had By All

and to that end it strives to widen the margin of leisure and extend the opportunities of enjoyment. But the very system that reduces the amount of work and increases the chances for diversion finds its problem merely shifted rather than solved, and more complicated than simplified. For fun and sport pall almost as promptly as toil and trouble, and devising means of amusement requires far more ingenuity than going through the motions of a routine job. But just as Utopia guards against too much of a bad thing by preventing overwork, it averts too much of a good thing by providing a generous but not extravagant allowance of leisure.

Moreover, it sees to it that leisure is not left vacant, neither perniciously filled. This precaution is the more necessary because of another curtailment—that of rest for the weary. Since in the life rational, people do not become abnormally fatigued, they need only a normal amount of repose. And since repose is the dullest use to which leisure may be put, this large quota of unoccupied time must be furnished with pleasurable activity.

This double shrinkage in allotment for work and for recuperation is stretched out again in Utopia by liberal indulgence in physical and esthetic recreation and in absorbing avocations, giving scope alike for social gregariousness and individual development. In ordinary life the pendulum swings from each level of labor to the corresponding level of release. But in Utopia there is neither the dreary oscillation from sodden drudgery to stupefied lethargy, nor much of the somewhat higher vibration from routine toil to the vicarious amusement that provides excitement without exertion. We do not find the Utopian population flocking to those thrilling spectacles that stimulate jaded senses without making annoying demands on either minds or muscles. It can worry along in the absence of melodramatic movies and jazzy revues, and it never is caught holding down the bleachers at ball-games or prize-fights. It is satisfied to react in a body from enjoyable work to enjoyable play, one as dynamic and purposeful as the other. In Campanella's Sun City, for another precedent, they "allow no game which is played while sitting."

But with all their unanimity as to the principle of recreation, the Utopians differ widely in their opinions about admissible types of amusement, actual proportions of labor and leisure, and so on. Some are too serious to concede much to what they consider the trifling side of life, others regard this side as means to the true end—productivity—rather than an end in itself, and certain are too Puritanical to countenance even the jest and youthful jollity approved by the greatest Puritan of them all. Even the urbane and convivial Sir Thomas More seemed to suppose that harkening to edifying lectures before breakfast and pottering about the garden after supper ought to be enough for the gayest dogs of Amaurot. His citizens might, however, travel about the island if they carried their passports and worked their way. And they had their monthly festivals called Cynemernes and Trapemernes.

Those who take diversion into account at all begin (and sometimes end) with turning the ordinary processes of living into delightful functions. Dining, for instance, is a daily commonplace that can easily be converted into an event of jocund mirth and gayety. Guests contribute the social element, company dishes the epicurean, and decorations the artistic. All the socialistic regimes make much of the communal dinner, panoplied with music, instructive discourse, reading aloud, and friendly conversation. The individualistic orders specialize in breakfast, dinner, or supper parties.

Bacon's Bensalemites celebrate the Feast of the Vine with majestic pomp and circumstance. But thereafter the French come to the front in this matter. Bretonne's Megapatagonians revel in prolonged Feasts of Marriages which make the most gorgeous carnivals of Europe look like poor shows. Thirion's Neustrians gather in three generations at the bountiful family feast that is sufficient reward for months of thrift and industry. In the same year, as it happens, Zola waxes eloquent over La Crècherie, whose jubilant commemorative summer festival concludes with its out-door sunset dinner. The various households have their meals separate but adjoining, and all gather closer for a municipal dessert. He describes it with lyric fervor:

"Thus one beheld the tables marching and uniting together in such wise that soon not a break remained along the avenues, before the doors of the gay houses. The Paschal feast of that brotherly people was about to continue under the stars, in a vast communion, all being seated elbow to elbow at the same board among the same scattered rose petals. The whole city thus became a gigantic banqueting hall, the families were blended into one, the same spirit animated every breast, and the same love made every heart beat."

Anatole France is not given to rhapsody even in his approvals, but he makes the chief episode in his brief Utopian sketch the lively table-talk of his cultured laborers. After dinner, if you are in Mercier's future Paris or Fox's New Holland or Chambless' Roadtown, you may spend the evening promenading along the fragrant blossoming roof-gardens which unite all the flat-topped houses of a street or form a bordering arcade.

Rustic picnics and outdoor sports are inevitable features of the idyllic life. In the Empire of Cantahar all are trained to be ambidextrous for greater flexibility in hunts, races, dances, and games; and these are organized into public festivals and spectacles. Even Fénelon's stern Telemachus encourages such entertainments at Salentum. In the southern elysium discovered by Jacques Sadeur the day is divided into three parts: Murc, from five to ten A. M., is devoted to public business and education; Durc, from ten A. M. to three P. M., to private business in field and shop; and Spurc, from three to eight P. M., to feats of skill and recreation.

Later in order we find the Sybarites and Ionians fond of hiking and swimming parties. The Freelanders glory in their riding and boating and skating. On the broad plateau above their city a six thousand acre lake is flooded to ballroom smoothness, and winter sports in Africa are carried on with the lavish magnificence that marks all their merry-makings. On Colymbia Island the ground is merely a spring-board for the aquatic life of this amphibian people, expert not only in fancy swimming but in under-water dancing, in shark-hunting and seal-racing. In Cooper's very practical Crater whale-fishing is a matter of profit, pleasure, and prestige; no youth is permitted to lead the dance until he has speared his leviathan. Saunders' Kalomera is another busy Utopia that skimps on its amusements. One week a year is given up to community festival, expanded to three weeks for the young people, and another three weeks for wedding-tours. The honeymoon, in fact, is specifically mentioned by many Utopians as the inalienable right of youth.

Music and dancing are naturally as popular within Utopia as without, serving both for recreation and for art. They abound everywhere, but the most notable modern instance is Merejkowski's Earthly Paradise, a return to the earlier idyllic Edens. These people are sophisticated in their simplicity. They have studied the past carefully and have consciously adopted the primitive life, divested of primitive cold, hunger, and fear, as the only ideal. By becoming as little children they enter the Kingdom of Happiness. They portion life into the three estates, work, joy, and wisdom. The first is occupied by Hottentot slaves, and the third by elderly sages. Both these groups live only to minister to the second, the period of joyful childhood, youth, and manhood. All concentrate on furthering the ecstatic glow of this truly golden mean of existence. For this middle span life is one endless round of feasting, playing, singing, and dancing, all in the open air, while the others supply their slight material wants on the one hand, and their moderate mental and emotional guidance on the other.

More original in their own time and prophetic of ours are the flying parties of the Vrilya and the Limanorans. To the former flight is possible through their detachable wings; to the latter by their transparent spirituel bodies. Stanley is the only Utopian to admit horse-racing but he prohibits gambling on it, and excludes hunting. Most modern and realistic is Jaeger's competitive athletics, in the novel form of mountain-racing. It is also the least sure of the idealistic status of sportsmanship.

The brooding skepticism indicated by the title of "The Question Mark" turns largely upon this doubtful blessing of superfluous time. Not superfluous for the Intellectuals, for what with their scientific research and creative artistry, their days are never long enough; but for the Normals, whose need for diversion and excitement is at once chronic and acute, yet never met by any inner resources. Dr. Wayland, his nephew John, and John's betrothed Sylvia Grant, have the serene and exultant mastery of life that comes from so blending work, play, and joy that they are not three things but one. But they are of the small minority whose minds are adequate to their experience. To the great majority belong Mrs. Wayland, bovinely placid when not mildly querulous and peevish, and her son and daughter, Terry the athlete and Ena the flapper, both restless, baffled, clamorous and defeated. The other Normals pacify themselves with their freakish fads, taking up exotic cults, establishing Oriental harems in British homes, collecting buttons and all such. But these two symbolize the frightful calamities that can spring from sheer emptiness, emptiness of hands and hearts and heads.

Ena's situation is the more tragic but Terry's better exemplifies the plight of having to do something without having something to do. The story shows two vivid pictures of this international champion: first as a conquering hero and swaggering cock of the walk, snuffing up the incense of adulation and glorying in power; second as an overgrown lout, loafing around home, bored and disgruntled, futilely petted by his emotional mother and contemptuously tolerated by his intellectual father. The immediate practical question is whether Terry shall register as an unskilled laborer, and continue to devote most of his time to the spectacular competitive mountain-racing that was the most popular diversion of the time and his own choice of an occupation, or train for some definite trade, as his father advised. In his "confused repinings" the distraught lad unconsciously expresses the unutopianism of Utopia.

"It isn't my fault," he argues, "that I haven't got brains. There's only one thing I can do, and that is mountain-racing; and that is just what he wants me to stop doing. Of course, I know he thinks racing is no use to anybody, but I don't see what that matters. Everyone knows that all the trades are overcrowded—they'll have to reduce the labor period soon. So why should I go when there are people who can't do anything else, and when everyone wants me to go on racing? If they were short of people it would be different; I'd go at once then and be glad to. . . . I don't see how you can say a thing is no use when it amuses people. If we can't afford to keep up our sport it seems to me a poor business. We might just as well be back in the twentieth century."

Terry's tirade may be a case of canny rationalizing, but for all that it rests on the perfectly sound principle that, since there is no accounting for tastes, and since the very essence of recreation is indulgence in one's particular taste, it is wise to recognise our human inequalities and to let us all get our pleasure the best way we can. Those who really prefer a fair amount of irresponsible drudgery which they can shed easily and from which they can shift joyfully into equally irresponsible amusement are as entitled to their likings as those who aspire to design their lives and prize leisure as the raw material out of which must be manufactured whatever they achieve.

It is the first class, the piece-mealers, Blatchford had in mind when he declared, "The average man is not ambitious, is not rapacious. He likes an easy and pleasant life and does not want to be bothered." It is the second class, the whole-clothers, referred to by another Utopian whose people are "avid of time not because rushed to death by nervous pressure, but because life is too rich in enjoyment to lose a moment." These are the scientific and artistic in spirit, if not professional scientists and artists, and they find their keenest delight not in being released from their fascinating labor but in returning to it, and they release themselves only for the relaxation and recreation necessary for getting on zestfully with the work in hand.

But for the most part the Utopian conception of play has more of the accepted and conventional in it than of the unique and inventive. Its general policy is passive, satisfied with insuring a harmonious milieu, a generous allowance of spare time, and an ample provision of the ordinary means of diversion, ruling out only those that bring a "morning after" in their train. Utopia follows the beaten path in supposing that if you take care of your work your play can take care of itself. Since wearing out is a more obvious process than rusting out, the penalties of over-exertion have been more carefully warded off than those of inaction.

If they think about it at all the Utopians are apt to stress the responsibility side of leisure. The reflective among them consider how man grew out of his primitive state of alternating rude toil with crude pleasure; how he came to demand extra accessories and embellishments that cost extra labor; how he paid this toll until it proved so irksome he fell upon the astute scheme of making the other fellow do the work and hand over the rewards; how this worked fine and evolved a civilization, and how this civilization turned around and asked what was being done with all that released time and energy and ability. To enjoy yourself in it is all very well up to a certain point. Beyond that point the idler becomes a sluggard and parasite, and these creatures are below par in the almost perfect State. It therefore increases the ratio of leisure time but advises that it be spent in the active, constructive kind of enjoyment, to the enhancement of both pleasure and profit.

The old exhortation to work while you work and play while you play becomes modified to play in your work and work at your play. For the higher the types of both, the more blurred becomes the line dividing them.

CHAPTER VI

BEAUTY AND ART

This pair of terms, only partly tautological, seems the best phrase to indicate Utopia's recognition of Nature's loveliness and Man's estheticism. The tribute paid is not large and some of it is rather perfunctory, but there is enough to give this subject a place in the sum of things. If the elusive intangible phenomenon called Beauty and the diverse indefinable efflorescence called Art are not preeminent, or even prominent, in our imaginary world, they are at least as taken for granted as education and recreation, and occasionally given the homage of a warm enthusiasm. For this world reflects the actual in revealing love of beauty as a primitive impulse and understanding of it as a mark of sophistication.

Yet the whole Utopian idea springs from a sense of the beauty in symmetry and cleanliness, the moral beauty of justice, the entrancement of general perfection. And some of the idealists have been aware of it.

"In the art of man," exclaims James Harrington, "there is nothing so like the first call of beautiful order out of chaos and confusion as the architecture of a well-ordered commonwealth." That the architecture of his own *Oceana* was forbiddingly dull and devious is only another negative answer to the question, "What hand and brain went ever paired?"

"The government of a kingdom," observes François Fénelon, "requires a certain harmony, like music, and just proportions, like architecture." But even in Utopia it is one thing to conceive and another to execute. Beauty itself is a perennial source of pleasure, and artistic creation the most joyous form of work-play. Yet since a cultivated taste is the only criterion of esthetic values, and the result of a training at once stiff and liberal, we are not astonished at certain Utopian exhibitions of the crude and gauche trying to be beautiful and succeeding in giving pleasure. Again there are flashes and gleams of genuine grace and memorable charm.

On the theme of natural beauty Utopians are the least expressive, not being a race of poets. In their artistry they begin, as with their recreation, by decorating and enhancing the uses and materials of daily life. Of these, the most easily manipulated is the costume. Clothes may not make the man but they certainly express his personality and indicate his status. In Utopia, however, all erratic individuality is standardized or muffled, for the prevailing tendency is to turn costumes into uniforms. Its citizens either dress alike to announce their perfect democracy or wear graded suits to signify their aristocracy.

To the first class belong the people discovered by Raphael Hythloday, and they are not merely negligent of adornment but disdainful of it. "Throughout the island they wear the same sort of clothes without any other distinction, except what is necessary to distinguish the two sexes, and the married and unmarried. The fashion never alters; and as it is neither disagreeable nor uneasy, so it is suited to the climate, and calculated both for their summers and winters." Each citizen has one working suit, of leather and skins, good for seven years, and one woolen upper garment, to be thrown over the other for public gatherings, good for two years. "Nor is there anything that can tempt a man to desire more; for if he had them, he would neither be the warmer nor would he make one jot the better appearance for it." For that reason silk is despised, gold made a badge of infamy, and jewels tossed as baubles to the children. Only the priestly vesture of parti-colored birds' plumage varies the monotony.

In sharp contrast to this is the high relish for color and pomp on the part of another British nobleman. Bacon is no follower of More. His shipwrecked explorer gazed with delight upon the rescuing Bensalemite and noted his glossy azure gown of water chamolet, completed with green tunic and turban. The second citizen to be observed was arrayed also in blue but with a red cross on his white turban and a tippet of fine linen. When a Father of Saloman's House made a stately entry into the city "He was clothed in a robe of fine black cloth and wide sleeves, and a cape: his under garment was of excellent white linen down to the foot, girt with a girdle of the same; and a sindon or tippet of the same about his neck. He had gloves that were curious, and set with stone; and shoes of peach-colored velvet. His hat was like a helmet, or Spanish montero." Preceding his cedar and crystal chariot bedecked with cloth-of-gold and sapphires and emeralds were fifty young men "all in white satin loose coats and stockings of white silk; and shoes of blue velvet; and hats of blue velvet, with fine plumes of divers colors, set round like hat-bands."

But except for the "most beautiful azure robes" worn by the judges in the Atlantis of Plato this colorful New Atlantis is an exception to the Utopian rule. In Christianopolis we understand that gray was worn every day and white for Sunday best. Fénelon's Hesperians were distinguished by a separate color for the seven classes of citizens and the no class slaves. The Ophirites used the same scheme on a simpler model. The greatest point of agreement among the later Utopians is the return to the Greek tunic and sandals. The neo-classic costume, often with a mention of gay and varied hues,

BEAUTY AND ART

is the fashion in Icaria, Freeland, Altruria, Nuiorc, Sonnenstadt, and many other places. Tardé's Undergrounders are unique in spun silver and gold and woven asbestos. Merejkowski alone discards all clothing in favor of the greater beauty of the nude.

Next in intimate closeness to the clothes a man wears is the house he lives in, and as capable of expressing his sense of beauty. But that sense in Utopia is manifested in civic buildings rather than individual homes. Its numerous circular cities with their radiating avenues and curving streets, the extensive mural decorations of the City of the Sun, the enormous handsome pillared arcade encircling the whole island of Altruria, serve to show how far from new is our boasted city-planning, and also testify to the creed that magnificence and splendor should be of community possession and enjoyment.

For this same reason household furnishing is dictated by science rather than by art. The principal place for furniture is in the home, and by the time you have subtracted from the Utopian home the luxury denied by its cult of simplicity, and added to it the sanitary equipment demanded by the cult of efficiency, the remainder left for artistic charm verges toward zero. By a curious paradox the only two places which suggest that a man's home, no longer needing to be his castle, might yet remain his palace, are the most undomestic of all. They are Lytton's subterranean realm and Sweven's mystic island, both featuring winged people who live much in the open air and care little for family life.

The upper-crust trespasser upon the underground Vrilya awakens from his first sleep to hear the warbling of birds trained to sing in concert, and to find himself in a silken luminous world. His room is hung and carpeted with a variegated fibrous matting, and commands a view of graceful plants and brilliant flowers in a hanging garden. Other apartments are "tesselated with spars, and metals, and uncut jewels." The air is filled with a delicious fragrance from sculptured golden censers.

The invader of Limanora likewise recovers consciousness in a world "of the most dazzling beauty." The walls and vaulted roof of the apartment gleam like a mosaic of lit jewelry. The floors shine with the colored radiance of a dew-belled meadow under the morning sun. The hangings are crystalline in their transparency and iridescence. Around the windows they form prismatic frames to glorious vistas without. A lucent plastic substance is molded into delicate lace-work or wrought into domes and arborescent columns as massive as marble. The spaciousness is broken by dignified arches, diversified by fragrant fountains, softened by warm nooks and cozy recesses. From unseen sources floats entrancing music. The dwellers themselves float, as they rest or converse, in alabaster-like chairs made flexible by air-cushions, and moved or suspended by means of electric batteries. It is a place of enchantment, though it seems to us more like a cathedral than a home.

To the epicurean there is no more gracious adornment of life than exquisite dining. And nowhere is the dinner table more the center of attraction than in Utopia. More's people "never sup without music; while they are at table, some burn perfumes and sprinkle about fragrant ointments and sweet waters: in short, they want nothing that may cheer up their spirits." Bacon's typical family feast is an elaborate affair. Campanella features music at meals, with the discreet provision that "only a few, however, sing; or there is one voice accompanying the lute and one for each other instrument." The women of this community have charge of all the music, and are permitted to paint pictures; but for a lady to paint her face or wear high heels or add a train to the Roman toga of the civic costume, is a capital crime.

It is mainly in this attention paid to the useful arts and in craftsmanship that Utopia expresses its esthetic sense. Save for music and dancing, which are prized more for their recreational functions than their artistic, the fine arts are not greatly patronized. The Megapatagonians despise painting and sculpture, consider drama childish, forbid all poetry except the ethical odes and epics which celebrate the deeds of humanity's benefactors, but they indulge freely in music and dancing. The Ionians agree that while theatrical performances are all right for children they are too silly to interest adults; yet they have miles of picture galleries. The Altrurians are also generous with art galleries and studios, and are fond of dancing and amateur theatricals. The Freelanders rate the stage as an educational forum, are particularly devoted to concerts, and care more for literature than any Utopians since Sir Thomas's originals, who themselves excel in religious music. It is indeed here, through the Crescent Islanders, that we have almost the only tribute to the emotional value of this art. Their singing "is so happily suited to every occasion that whether the subject of the hymn be cheerful or formed to soothe or trouble the mind, or to express grief or remorse, the music takes the impression of whatever is represented, affects and kindles the passions, and works the sentiments deep into the hearts of the hearers." And even the staid Christianopolites have their choral dances and their sacred dramas to celebrate each of the four seasons.

In spite of the fact that Art in Utopia is more implicit than explicit, Utopia resembles Art in being a product of the imagination and a reaching toward perfection. If this were a genuine kinship it might be manifested by a large proportion of Utopias imbued thoroughly with the artistic spirit. Since it is only an accidental connection, it is a small proportion that we find so animated. The fantastic Mercurians are called specialists in humor and beauty. The idyllic Megapatagonians are described as concentrating on teachers and artists, being too peaceable to need lawyers, too healthy to need physicians, and too sensible to need preachers. Lytton and Sweven are the only ones to speak of the spiritual and intellectual beauty in the faces of their perfected people, and this is the more interesting because of the contrast between the static temperament of the Vrilya and the dynamic disposition of the Limanorans.

The only artist on the creator list is William Morris but his Utopian creation takes it out on "work-pleasure,"—the farmer carving his own pipe and the barefoot girl embroidering her silk gown. To these Medievalists projected into the future, the satisfaction of shaping and enjoying something beautiful is "the wages God gets." This sentiment is echoed by Robert Blatchford, who agrees that art is for life's sake and that fine living is the finest art. As late as 1920 we find a bit of reactionary naiveté in Richmond's picture of the placid family group spending an evening at home in the shelter of their clean quiet octagonal walled city, father and son constructing a table, mother at her loom, daughters sewing their blue woolen dresses with strong waxed thread.

It was left to Gabriel Tarde, a Professor of Political Economy, to evoke the only truly artistic people in all Utopia. His Underground Neo-Troglodytes of the far future are absorbed, not in the utilitarian craft that ornaments the implements of living, but the pure art that is for its own sake. Their guilds of artists and scientists live apart in their own cities. And since their population must be rigorously restricted, elimination is made by the esthetic test. Artistic ability is a prerequisite to parenthood. No man may produce a child until he has produced a work of art, the worth of this to be adjudged by his rivals. And for every succeeding child there must be a new work of art. This policy flows from their creed that in art is the only real aristocracy, for "the lower orders produce only to consume, the higher consume only to produce." This is the relative ranking because "to produce is a passion, to consume is only a taste." Civilization is attained when we have "a minimum of utilitarian work and a maximum of esthetic." The value of such a society is that it "reposes, not on the exchange of services, but on the exchange of admiration or criticism."

It would be more accurate to say that this lofty culture is rooted in the exchange of services that marks all human society, but that it blooms in a mutual appreciation of its highest productions. Certainly it is this blossoming into fervent regard for beauty and into the art that captures beauty through genius, which gives any society, Utopian or otherwise, the proud status of superiority, going on perfection. But the flower must have a stem, and the stem a stock, and the stock a root, and the root a seed, and the seed its soil and favorable conditions for sprouting. It is only because constrained by necessity that the Utopians have kept their eyes on the entire process instead of fastening it solely on the culmination. After the trick of flower-production is once learned, multiplication of the product will be comparatively easy.

But if it is natural that the Utopians should have been more preoccupied with the Just and the Good than the Beautiful, and should have promoted the useful arts more than the pure, in their own artless belief in art for life's sake, it is also inevitable that the moderns should begin to rank beauty and art as the higher necessities. Now that the foundations of practical idealism have been laid, its esthetic columns and towers may ascend and aspire.

CHAPTER VII

RELIGION AND MORALITY

THE remark that the two things requisite for making a Utopia are religion and a small country is no longer applicable. Utopias are getting to be as big as all out doors, and yet in all that space they are devoting little room to the paraphernalia of public worship. The earlier communities were indeed restricted and pious, even to being avowed theocracies. And as they reflected the religious fervor and orthodox beliefs of their times, so the later ones parallel the modern indifference and eclecticism.

Nor is there anything extraordinary about their ethical standards. These idealists do no more than represent as being in actual practice the precepts already current and theoretically accepted. For most of the Utopians are laymen in this field also. There are not many more theologians among them than artists, and they are as innocent of technical instruction in ethics as in esthetics. Few of them make any distinction between religion and morality, but go on the traditional assumption that they are practically synonymous.

Plato, it is true, is concerned primarily with the

virtues of an ideal State, and would trim the Greek mythology until it tallied with the moral needs of youth. But among those virtues he did not include truth in either sense of the word; his highest regard was not reserved for either verity or veracity. These are all very well so long as they are kept in their place. "Since a lie is useless to the gods," says Socrates, "and useful only as a medicine to men, then the use of such medicines should be restricted to physicians." The rulers may be allowed to lie for the public good, but anyone else caught in mendacity is to be severely punished. This is in accord with a system that exalts obedience, temperance, courage, and sagacity as the virtuous hierarchy. The Atlantans, described in *Critias*, were descended from the god Poseidon, to whom was erected a magnificent temple. "As long as the divine nature lasted in them, they were obedient to the laws, and well-affectioned towards the gods, who were their kinsmen; for they possessed true and in every way great spirits, practising gentleness and wisdom in the various chances of life, and in their intercourse with one another." But alas, this divine nature became diluted with its mortal admixture, and when finally human nature got the upper hand, that was the end of them.

The human nature portrayed by More shows a curious advance upon one phase of his own character. This zealous Churchman who would exterminate heretics, and who kept his own faith to the extent of a blithely endured martyrdom, is particularly emphatic over the liberal doctrine of his idealized people. They are theists who permit sun-worship and hero-worship, allow no religious persecution, and countenance only a persuasive proselyting. Recognizing that belief in a creed is not an optional matter, they make no discrimination except to rule that unbelievers in God and immortality may not hold office, be given any public trust, or suffered to argue before the common and too pliable populace. Although they despise superstition they hold that the souls of the dead are present invisibly among the living; and they find the Catholicism of their visitors so congenial that many are converted to it. Their priests have no political power but tremendous moral influence. No punishment is more dreaded than ostracism from the temple. Sir Thomas evidently saw no inconsistency in adding that the wicked who do not very quickly satisfy the priests of their repentance are seized on by the Senate and punished for their impiety; and that the clergy themselves are immune. "If they should happen to commit any crime, they would not be questioned for it; for they do not think it lawful to lay hands on any man, how wicked soever he is, that has been in a peculiar manner dedicated to God." Since the future life holds retribution for vice, the due penalty is merely deferred. As for virtue being its own reward, it is so far from it as to be "a sour and difficult thing." To renounce the pleasures of life, and undergo pain and trouble, except for the prospect of a reward, they reckon "the maddest thing in the world."

Yet they are so preoccupied with ethics that among their few games is one which "resembles a battle between the virtues and the vices, in which the enmity in the vices among themselves, and their agreement against virtue, is not unpleasantly represented; together with the special oppositions between the particular virtues and vices; as also the methods by which vice either openly assaults or secretly undermines virtue; and virtue on the other hand resists it." Their ethical philosophy is decidedly and thoroughly hedonistic, a hedonism that admits the sensuous but stresses the intellectual and spiritual. They realize the utilitarian basis of altruistic service, and even such professional public benefactors as the Brutheskas are frank to acknowledge the ultimately egoistic nature of their motives.

Bacon's scientific Bensalemites were already devout Christians, for about the middle of the first century they had been "saved from infidelity (as the remain of the old world was from water) by an ark, through the apostolical and miraculous evangelism of St. Bartholomew." The Solopolites in their allegoric way name the civic magistrates after their favorite virtues. Among their officials are Magnanimity, Fortitude, Chastity, Justice, Comfort, Truth, Kindness, Gratitude, Cheerfulness, Exercise, and Sobriety. Of the vices they count pride the worst. Campanella has considerable to say about the forms of worship, and Andreae says his Christianopolis was "founded by Religion, an Exile from Europe": but neither the Protestant clergyman nor the Catholic monk pays higher tribute to religion than do these two British laymen, More and Bacon.

More completely theologic than any are the Teutonic Felsenburg Island and Kingdom of Ophir. In the former the pastor could preach for two solid hours without beginning to weary his congregation or himself. In the latter the crown prince is occupied in supervising the clergy, and the king pledges himself to lead a godly life and support the Christian faith. No citizen may be unequally yoked with an unbeliever. Yet proselyting is discouraged and tolerance encouraged. Prophets and soothsayers are banished, sermons and rituals strictly censored. Hymns and tunes may be "pathetic but not theatrical." The ethical spirit is expressed in an eloquent symbolism. The kingdom is named from the ancient Ophir whence were brought gold and silver, ivory, apes, and peacocks, for the adornment of Solomon's Temple. If, says the anonymous author, anyone wishes to know the location of this later namesake, let him take this information:

"Where the true Christian religion, with its

RELIGION AND MORALITY

teaching and the godly mode of life alike of the teacher and the listener, goes diligently forward, there is the purest virgin gold; where right and justice are impartially administered, there is the finest silver; where upright conduct is in goodly blossom, there is the ivory which brings profit to many; where subjects see naught before them save the Christlike actions of their ruler, there are the finest apes; where all the royal servants work faithfully and untiringly for the welfare of their master and the attainment of the common weal, there are the most vigilant peacocks; and where all this exists, there is the Kingdom of Ophir."

These and still later Utopias reflect an era when secular rulers were by the same token Defenders of the Faith. Baxter's Holy Commonwealth is firmly guided by patrician patriarchs, a policy necessary because "the major part of the vulgar are scarcely prudent and pious men, and the rabble hate restraint and reason." Gott's Regained Jerusalem does not lag behind in doctrine and holiness. Harrington advocates a national religion with choice in form of worship to all except Pagans, Papists, and Jews. The universities of his Oceana bestow their highest honors upon the theologians, yet these ecclesiastics are not encouraged to meddle in the government, where "an ounce of wisdom is worth a pound of clergy."

In passing from the seventeenth to the eighteenth

century this particular topic seems to move from England to France. Fénelon's *Télémaque* aims to make people happy through piety and virtue. Varennes de Mondasse has his Cantahar founded by a humanized angel, Saranki, who inculcated a worship of the sun, moon, and stars. The sun, Monski, judges the souls of the newly dead. With a touch of Greek mythology he promotes the good to be fixed and shining stars, but is more inventive in turning the bad into falling stars, the sight of whose descent is calculated to frighten still living souls into proper behavior. Also as in the Hades and Inferno legends, these sinners must wander and suffer each according to his own wickedness. A dramatic episode in the story tells of the danger in which the visitor is placed by his refusal to be impressed by a solar eclipse and become a convert to this heliac cult. There is, however, an ironic tone in the recital of this heterodox stranger's stubborn adherence to his native faith that turns the satire against narrow dogmatism. The tale contains also a long argument on the advantage of an authorized state religion; it discusses the desirability of an unascetic monastic life for any citizen over thirty who might wish to become a recluse on a moderate pension; and it describes, as do so many of the Utopias, a funeral celebrated with joyful obsequies. The ideal religion does not permit lugubrious mourning over the dead, since death is but the passage from a relative to an absolute perfection.

The more liberal theology of the French merges naturally into a wide agnostic freedom. In the anonymous Monde d'Mercure a broad theism prevails, which sets the style for Mercier's future Paris as well as Bellamy's future Boston. Fontenelle's Ajaonier claims no founder of either Church or State, and is thus relieved of political parties and denominational sects. Nature is the Divine Mother and the Golden Rule the only law. In Bretonne's Megapatagonia "pleasure is considered the most efficacious manner of honoring the Deity." The Italian Mantegazza thinks that by the year 3000 all creeds will be dwelling in fraternal amity, and that conspicuous among the churches will be a Temple of Hope.

By the nineteenth century Utopians everywhere are content with paying vague respects to the supernatural where they do not actually distrust it. Already Berington's Mezzoranians had forbidden religious discussion, and in Maitland's sweet By and By all dogma is prohibited as positively immoral. With sly irony Lytton commends the Vrilya for really believing and practising their liberal creed, and explains that this sincerity results from the lack of formal organization. Cooper shows how smoothly the Crater progresses as long as the whole community is shepherded by one non-sectarian pastor, and how quickly it goes to smash once the serpent of dissension sneaks into the garden and sets the rival churches to competing and quarrelling, so that simple piety is strangled by mutual jealousy and hatred.

The only modern Utopia to stress theology at all is Saunders' Kalomera. Here we find a philosophic race vitally influenced by its own religious faith because that is a doctrine of voluntary cooperation between humanity and divinity in the great evolutionary plan. All who enter this crusade to promote the design of the First Cause, Elomusa, become Elomusami, the spiritual aristocracy. The lazy and selfish naturally exclude themselves. The central building of each city is a church where on their Sabiom, a sort of ethical Sabbath, services are conducted Quaker style, popular gatherings for calm meditation or informal conference without interference of clergy. They expect no personal immortality but are content to further the kingdom of heaven on earth.

With even less use for ecclesiasticism, Sweven's Limanorans are more passionately imbued with spiritual fire than any Utopian people. At one stage in their history they purged their island of its undesirable citizens by buying them out and shipping them to more congenial climes. After the deportation was accomplished, they discovered it had swept away the priests along with the politicians and other baneful nuisances. The evicted, who later formed the Rialleran exiles, consisted of "the lying and hypocritical, the licentious, the envious and jealous, the boastful and the epicurean, the religiously intolerant and superstitious, the warlike and murderous, and the thievish and socialistic." This major operation being safely over, they followed it up by a vigorous national cleansing for the removal of any lingering contamination. With exultant gusto they eradicated "the seedling ferocities of their savage past: spite, rancor, disdain, pitilessness, vanity, surliness, ingratitude, partiality, want of candor, acerbity, meanness, and all uncharitableness."

In the process, however, they found this constant feeling of their moral pulse to be breeding a morbid hypochondria, and were warned by the symptoms of timid modesty and flabby philanthropy that they were disintegrating. Whereupon they tried a regimen of physical culture and material science until their superb athletic prowess and miraculous inventions brought on the malady of complacent arrogance. Thus finally they were brought to comprehend that for their own health, sanity, and happiness an external interest was required, a definite yet unreachable goal, capable of enlisting the interest and absorbing the energy of a noble and talented people. Nothing could qualify for this but devotion to racial progress. Hence their conclusion, which became also their principle of action and criterion of behavior: "Morality is the effort to adapt conduct and ideals to the new vistas opened up into the future by an advance already achieved. Evil is the past which has become so obsolete and is yet so living as to be obstructive. Whatsoever dallies with an outgrown principle or element is immoral."

This racial obligation must, moreover, be self-determined and spontaneous, because to be parasitic or even dependent is also immoral, and all proselyting, evangelism, or uplifting is pernicious to everybody concerned. This disposal of criminals as social invalids, to be cured or segregated, and the diagnosis of sinners as figments of the theological imagination, sounds more scientific than spiritual, but the Limanorans expressly disclaim being irreligious. After the clerical exodus the community observed with some astonishment that when ecclesiasticism went out true religion came in, and thereupon they deduced the idea that "the surest way to exclude religion from life is to assign to it a special section of time, a special profession, and special edifices." For all these act as a conduit that withdraws piety and aspiration from ordinary existence. Removing the conduit, so far from destroying religion, floods it through all life with a sort of permeating pantheism. Creeds and codifications must be discarded because "nothing encased in a mold can grow," and growth is the only morality. To accept any inspiration as final is to offend against the Ultimate, and such offense is the only infidelity. "The devil is the spirit of stagnancy and retrogression." To counteract his malign influence is to worship whatever gods there be, saying it with deeds instead of words. In spite of their unreality these fervent etherial people are the best exponents of our own Zeitgeist in their objective religion and kinetic morality. By their code religion is divorced from theology and wedded to sociology. And morality has suffered a sea-change from a conservative to a radical status. The traditional virtues of obedience, meekness, conformity, and resignation, have degenerated into vices. The former vices of rebellion, assertiveness, initiative, and discontent, have been elevated to virtues. The old ethical antithesis between right and wrong, good and bad, have become transformed into the new (or rather, revived) intellectual opposition between wise and foolish, intelligent and stupid.

The same year happened to bring forth this scientific spirituality of the Scot and the Russian neo-deism. In Merejkowski's Earthly Paradise the people are too happy to believe in an interfering deity who must be propitiated, but this happiness is grounded in the precepts of their own commonsense codified into the Ten Commandments of reason. In effect this is the Decalogue in which they trust and on which they act:

1 Become as little children.
2 Observe the golden mean in pleasure.
3 Live simply and frugally and, for that purpose, in the tropics.
4 Love and obey the Guardians.
5 Work not for your daily bread. Let the slaves do it.
6 Desire no progress.
7 Multiply only by selected breeding for race welfare.
8 Oppose not evil. Let it defeat itself.
9 Be happy in beauty and beautiful through happiness.
10 Be not troubled over death nor anticipate its terror.

On Simpson's Mars the religious situation is a combination of human participation in divine teleology and the esthetic cult of beauty. State and Church join in a jubilant theism which has no room for either charity or crime. Instead of sermonizing about duty the leaders offer large rewards for virtue. William Stanley foresees an enlightened faith, conscious of the anthropological and historical aspects of religion. By a curious reversion, the Dream City of "Unitas," dreamed of in 1920, harks back to a Christian Theocracy. Paul Adam's Franco-Borneans also used the Christian symbolism but with evolutionary interpretations in their mystic creed.

Strangely enough, it is in a still later Utopia that we find a return to subjective religion and static morality, but it is projected as a concession to mortal psychology. The real crook in Jaeger's Question Mark is the capacity of human nature for rational living. The population of that future London is divided into the Intellectuals and the Normals, the latter of course being the Emotionals. These constitute the great majority who always will need a charm against fear, an outlet for sensuous cravings, and an opening into regions of the mystic and occult. This need is crystallized in the wide magnetic supremacy of Father Emmanuel, and his ultimate sad fate represents the dilemma encountered when the human dependence upon comfort and blessed assurance finds its inner resources hollow and its outer reliance illusory.

Perhaps the most fitting names for the horns of the religious dilemma are dogma and materialism. The horn of dogma is triumphantly mounted and ridden by Robert Benson in his *Dawn of All,* which presents the grand apotheosis of Catholicism, made the more effective by its diametric contrast in his companion-piece, *Lord of the World.* The horn of materialism is mastered by the general Utopian trust in racial perfectibility. The human race may look like a dubious proposition to take much stock in, with very few preferred shares or gilt-edged securities, but that only makes it all the more exciting to take a chance. In its devotion to a spiritualized humanism Utopia is fundamentally religious and unimpeachably moral.

CHAPTER VIII

DOMESTICITY

A HOUSE to house canvass to see what the Utopians are doing about the home reveals an untoward state of affairs. In this realm of the perfectionists our Home Sweet Home with all its wealth of emotional romance and tender sentiment is disposed of quite summarily. Sometimes it is relegated to a back seat, sometimes ignored, sometimes deliberately ousted. Whether or not there is no place like home, certainly there is nothing like some of the homes in Utopia.

Over to the left, in the socialistic section, the personal household is abolished or subordinated to the communal type. And even in the individual branch, what they point to with pride is not so much the home itself as the oil on its machinery; what they boast of most thankfully is their escape from domestic shackles and tyranny. This is not to say that the Utopians consciously or unanimously repudiate the family as a social group. The problem involved is unusually baffling because of its heterogeneous elements. Based on the most intimate and vital relationships, the home must be concerned also with the most mundane and utilitarian of human interests. With the first of these aspects, the personal and emotional, State Makers do not feel called upon to deal, as it lies outside of their scope if not of their capacity. And the second offers enough points of attack to engage all the reformer's attention and enlist all of his ingenuity. For what with its economic, industrial, social, and other factors, the home is an institution of unlimited possibilities. Yet in reality so few of these have been made good that this institution stands to be convicted of hiding its talents or wasting them.

Aside from the principle of taking away even that which he hath from an unprofitable servant, there is the patriotic policy that regards as paramount the welfare of the State. The personnel of this wing has a low opinion of the home as a citizen-factory, and therefore advocates taking the children in hand while they are very young and giving the pliant twigs the proper bent. Moreover, with the youngsters out of the way, the domestic regime is greatly simplified and the adults released for doing their share of the community's productive work.

Efficiency also demands communal kitchens, mess-halls, laundries, in place of the futile and expensive makeshifts that render the individual household an unwarrantable extravagance. With all this enlargement of the domestic unit, however, only a few recommend pure communism. And those who do follow Plato and the other Greeks in abolishing the home are among the minor French prophets. Bretonne presents Habitations holding one hundred each, and d'Alais stretches his Osmasia to one thousand, both anticipating the Phalansteries of Fourier. At the other extreme is Sweven, with his ratio of one child to each lonesome Limanoran household, and that one in charge of the proparents chosen for euthenics as the real parents are for eugenics.

The compromise established by More has been a favorite ever since. The Crescent Islanders dine in company but each family has its own dwelling. Country families consist of at least forty members and two slaves. Every year twenty of these are exchanged for twenty urbanites, so that all have a two year term at husbandry. The size of the city families ranges from ten to sixteen members, the number being equalized by a transfer of excess children to deficient households. Each household is a patriarchy of three generations, the women "marrying out." Thirty of these families constitute a ward, at whose central hall they assemble for meals. This arrangement is not compulsory; "for though any that will may eat at home, yet none does it willingly, since it is both ridiculous and foolish for any to give themselves the trouble to make ready an ill dinner at home, when there is a much more plentiful one made ready for him so near at hand." These meals are prepared by the women, taking turns, and are served by the juveniles from six to the time of marriage. The younger children are by themselves in charge of nurses. From these orderly and convivial tables the citizens scatter by day to their work and at night to their stereotyped houses, with no keys in the doors. But to prevent undue attachment to these domiciles as near alike as peas in a pod, their inhabitants are compelled to rotate by lot every decade.

The Christianopolites are more stable and more modern. Their residence section is also three storied but is built on the apartment house plan, the cozy little three-room flats being connected by balconies and arcades. The limited space is sufficient because the children are bestowed in the civic dormitories, the food is brought in from the public stores, and the dinner limited to four dishes, "seasoned with wise and pious words." These simple folk are nevertheless provided with furnace heat, plumbing, ventilation, quarantine, and general sanitation. In the Sun City the two-meal-a-day habit, with much attention paid to diet and other hygienic rules prolongs life to upwards of a century.

After this pioneering the succeeding specific references to the home consist mainly of more of the same, brought up to date by adoption of labor-saving devices and all sorts of automatic conveniences. The New Britainers carry the domestic atmosphere even into jail, where each inmate has a suite of two rooms and does light housekeeping. Hale echoes More's slogan of "no house without a garden," but reduces the three stories to one, forecasting the bungalow. His Sybarites have individual homes, but sometimes four families take a block-sized lot together and build a combination residence unit, with common cuisine, library, and playground. Jules Verne in his France-Ville, located in Oregon, also votes for the garden-girt home, limited to two stories but completely equipped with the latest in sanitation; while Anatole France has a fancy for "small smiling pink cottages," supplemented by "large palatial dining-halls," where the prepared concentrated food is served in handy little cubes, with an exception in favor of real cheese and beer. Howells specializes in mushrooms, used freely to flavor a strict vegetarian diet.

Saunders describes with minute detail the Kalomeran apartment houses, constructed of steel, terra cotta, and papier-mâché, built Roman fashion around a central open court. Each structure accommodates two dozen families who live in a sort of compromise between private quarters and communal dormitories. Housework is done cooperatively by the women with assistance from the young people. Stanley is another to dwell fondly on the advantages of club life, made even more convenient by the addition of guild features. Birds of an industrial feather flock together in these buildings, which vary from the simple and modest to the grand and palatial in size and furnishings. They are prevalent in city suburbs and isolated villages. The Merchants' Clerks' Club is described as a sample:

"There are about two thousand apartments in this building, and it is by no means one of the largest. We enter a spacious marble hall, which forms a primary reception room. To the left we have the library and reading rooms, and a few small private conversation rooms. Beyond we have the billiard rooms. Through the front doorway we may see the dining rooms and breakfast rooms. To the right there is a large drawing room, and beyond, a music room, with a small theater. At the back we have pleasure grounds, a gymnasium and swimming baths." For membership references are required and continued good behavior is demanded, the more important as the club is a permanent residence and not merely a social center.

But with all these variations, whether the family itself is considered the unit or only a fraction of the communal unit, it is the biological group consisting of husband and wife and children that forms the nucleus of Utopia's standard orthodox home. Very few venture out to either extreme. The extreme of compulsion, where all mating and breeding are dictated and regulated by the government, is reached at rare intervals and represented by Campanella in the seventeenth century, Restif de la Bretonne in the eighteenth, and Paul Adam in the nineteenth. The extreme of liberty has an equally scant support by such as Claude Gilbert, L. B. Hellenbach, F. E. Bilz, and the anonymous author of *Colymbia*.

These extremists are, however, all and equally convinced of the righteousness of their respective systems. Those by whom marriages are made in the State House count racial welfare as the supreme consideration, and believe the individual well sacrificed to society. For them the divine principle is hygiene, and the prime feminine virtue is not chastity but fecundity. But the scientific hardness of this doctrine is softened and decorated by the artistry of gala courtships and ceremonial betrothals. In *The Flying Man* is portrayed the annual festivity, lasting a whole month, in which the year's crop of adolescents are paired off on biennial contracts. The most beautiful are awarded to the bravest, since "woman is made for man as man is made for the country," but all are provided for, and in this tandem monogamy each lady is sure of her due succession of husbands. In *Lettres de Malaisie* we have a vivid picture of the City of Diana, where all youths just out of school are assembled for a fortnight of merriment and promiscuity, with every encouragement to mate. The pregnant girls are then transferred to the Palace of Mothers. Thereafter they may go at intervals to the City of Venus but never again to Diana. The pregnant period is one of the utmost honor and adulation. The expectant mother is a royal creature who must have the best of everything. Throughout her maternal career she acquires a new gold button for every child. Every woman is at the desire of every man and never thinks of refusing the courtesy. This is no hardship, since all wooers are young, healthy, and comely. All men over forty live in retreats called Presbyteries. Next to the mothers in distinction and reward are the physicians who study to make child-birth easier.

For the proponents of individualism to the point of free love the most eloquent spokesman is Hellenbach. In his Mellonta there is no more chaperonage for maidens than for youths, on the principle that "no one has any right to know what goes on in the hearts and the dwellings of young girls." At the age of fifteen every lad and every maid is given a room which is the owner's castle. When babies are born, always of course strong and beautiful, they are given a temporary name by the mother, for which an official name is substituted when the child is fifteen. All women who are not mothers at twenty-two are known as Bacchabtin.

It is natural enough that only the minority report should declare for abrogation of the marriage tie and complete equality of the sexes, whether on the basis of free love or state control, even though the latter policy has its high precedent in Plato the pioneer. Although the pagan Greek was in advance of his own time, he did not run directly counter to it. But Western Utopias from the Renaissance on down have been under the spell of Medieval chivalry and sacerdotalism; seeing no anomaly in the cult of slave-worship, and feeling unsafe unless God and the priest blessed our home. Accordingly marriage at a reasonably early age is taken for granted, if not enforced; and even though personal choice is allowed, it is hedged about by many requirements and restrictions. One of the most important of these is the specification as to marriageable ages for grooms and brides respectively.

Thomas More makes it twenty-two and eighteen, and adds a provision for each of the contracting parties to view the person of the other, in the company of a grave matron and elder, as a preventive against concealment of blemishes or deformities. Andreae names twenty-four and eighteen as ideal ages, while Mondasse pushes it up to twenty-five and eighteen. The latter's Kingdom of Cantahar was originally polygamous but was manoeuvered by the women into monogamy. It features also the public courtship, begun at the annual spring festival, when all new candidates are registered and introduced to one another. During the next six months the youths inform the officials of their choices, which must be confined to girls of their own social class. Dowry is paid by the men, the price being in proportion to the ladies' loveliness. By a neat financial adjustment, the money paid into the public coffer for beautiful brides is turned over to the homely virgins who are forced to marry penniless lads, the dowry thus finally passing from a tax to a bonus. At the end of this half year of match-making, all reassemble at a harvest-home party, and here the maidens are permitted a limited expression of preference by being given a list of their own choosers and choosing from that. This is followed by the official announcement and pairing-off. Each swain presents his lass with a heart-shaped flower, goes through the wedding ceremony in the temple, and leads her home. Thus all women are provided with husbands, the poor and plain having the compensation, says the author, of a tranquillity denied to the wealthy and beautiful. Any wife who suspects her husband of waning interest and strayed affections is admonished to look to herself rather than to him for the cause, and to study to win him back instead of venting futile reproaches. Divorce may, however, be secured by a cogent appeal to the tribunal, which is composed of both men and women. Men may remain unmarried on payment of a bachelor's tax.

Among the more modern, Cabet fixes the ideal

marriage at twenty and eighteen, Craig at twenty-five and twenty-two, Stanley at twenty-four and eighteen. As the voice of the growing insistence on eugenic and other qualifications, William Stanley is the most explicit. His portrait of the 1950 bridegroom is drawn with a number of strokes: "He must be of good constitution and in good health. He should not be of the idler class. He should possess a good character, and never have been convicted of crime or drunkenness. He should have passed a certain standard of education in a public or a licensed school. He should possess not less than fifty pounds in the savings bank." The woman is not inferior at any point except that she can do with twenty pounds and a knowledge of domestic economy and hygiene.

Not only marriage but monogamy is sanctioned by the majority of our idealists. A touch of Mormonism occurs in Ajaonier, the oriental archipelago which consists of six circular islands, each circle containing one city and six villages, each village mustering twenty families, and each family composed of one husband, two wives, the children under five, and enough slaves to do the work. The duality in wives is for the purpose of keeping them keyed up to the best conjugal behavior through the spur of jealous rivalry. Marriage is compulsory for all men over twenty, and here also it follows a ceremonial public courtship.

Authorized polygamy is even rarer than no marriage at all. The two most notable instances of it feature it as a means of racial improvement. In Merejkowski's Earthly Paradise it seems that about thirty years before the story opens the slow rate of progress had been speeded up by the arrival from a neighboring isle of a perfect Adonis who gave the racial stock a great boost by becoming the husband of all the women of that generation, and father of all the children of the present. At one time the population had been reduced to twenty-five men and six hundred women, all superior, the inferior having been exterminated by race-suicide in the race toward perfectibility. Hauptmann may have borrowed this idea for his own idyllic Island of the Great Mother, which was populated by the one mysterious beautiful father.

Since it is Utopia's program to make everybody feel contented in a world where there is enough justice and other luxuries to go around, the lot of Woman is given some special attention. But the nature and amount of feminine freedom and equality depend as much as other items on the program-maker's personal bias. The general impression given is of a noble intent to ameliorate, modified by a conviction that this improvement must be a cautious and deliberate affair.

Woman as a petted plaything is found—where it might be expected—in an African and a South

American paradise. The dames of Mezzorania, idling in the scented silken suites of their monogamous harems, are "given enough freedom to keep them good-natured." The Megapatagonian matrons have heavier responsibilities. They must become expert in adornment, learn to dance gracefully, and practise the pleasant smile, in order to keep the men good-natured.

More stern and scrupulous in appearance although perhaps no more strictly dominated, is the fate of the girls of Ophir, for they are "educated in the religious virtues, and in domestic knowledge by the widows of pastors in their homes." Yet even these disciplined damsels are not allowed to "grow altogether shy and gloomy," as they must be made into cheerful brides for schoolmasters and clergymen. This leaden Utopia is, however, an exception. The exception in the form of drastic regulation is found in the benign Altruria, where the authorities are cruel to the extent of requiring a year of betrothal spent in a probationary separation.

There is less sentimentalizing over women in Utopia than might be expected. Almost the only gushing rhapsody comes from Robert Blatchford, as he eulogizes the "flower-sweet and heavenly-wise mother, whose breast is the cradle of all womanhood and manhood, whose immeasurable love and matchless intuition win the reverence of the wise." It is appropriate that in a Sorcery Shop a lovely lady should produce as by magic a delectable luncheon for extemporaneous guests. Woman in this future Manchester, as she "dispenses her healing tenderness and purifying graces," is at once queen bee and butterfly.

In Freeland, another African province, she is more bee than butterfly but still queen. While all able-bodied men must work, a maintenance sum amounting to about half salary is paid from the public treasury to invalids, the aged, children and women. This last subsidy is voted on the ground that women pay their way by being ornaments and supervisors of the home, and by making all life more gracious and beautiful. The most notably efficient housekeepers among them are elected to be the adopted mother-teachers of young girls, and this is reckoned a great honor, somewhat as in Ophir and Kalomera and the Dream City. All other occupations are open to those who have special tastes and talents, and the two professions of teaching and nursing are encouraged. Housework itself is ranked as a paid profession in a number of the modern Utopias, Taylor's Intermere, for instance, and all of Rosewater's fantasies. The significance of this is that as the status of the home decreases the status of the home-maker increases.

It is not that woman is felt to be promoted from home-making to higher and finer careers, since there is no such thing, but that home-making itself is promoted to the dignity of a remunerative career. As soon as that happens, men are willing to be caught at it and take a hand in it. Household engineering thus assumes the prestige of any superior vocation.

The women who have most conspicuously come out of the kitchen are of the futuristic class: Anatole France foresees women workers in blouse and breeches. Bellamy's Edith Leete on the edge of the twenty-first century is proud as Lucifer of her job. Thiusen's Ialma and Ulmene in the ninety-sixth century do their four-hour daily stunt in their home shop, between the hasty early bite and the late leisurely family breakfast. And if, among these gentle Diothas, a woman should wish to become a Zerata and devote herself to scientific research, she could have a better time even than intellectual Zee of the Vrilya college. Luxurious clubs are at her disposal, lavishly equipped with libraries and laboratories, besides the special Medical College for women.

But however exalted the position of woman in man's world, it is still man's world which she inhabits by his sufferance and on his terms. It is only in her own world, the Matriarchy, that she really queens it, but here she reigns in royal fashion. There is enough of this feminine dominance in Utopia to form a little suburb by itself, chronologically a newly opened tract, although there is a faint prelude as far back as the fourteenth century in a romance by Peter de Bosco.

About sixty years ago Lytton portrayed a "Coming Race" whose women excelled the men in physique, and took the initiative in courtship and proposing marriage. They also took their husbands on a three year probation, thus standardizing the trial marriages in vogue among the Mercurians. But once married, these Gyei voluntarily turned the tables on themselves and became model faithful and docile wives, in the four thousand superior families, symbolizing their domestic state by relinquishing their wings. They indicated their position and attitude also by an expressive color scheme. A young Gy wearing red thereby signified that she still preferred her maiden meditations fancy free; in gray, that she was looking around for a spouse; in purple, that she had made her choice; in orange, that she was betrothed; in blue, that she was divorced or widowed and ready for another trial. The men, called Ana, had the privilege of taking a second wife at the end of ten years, but this nominal polygamy was seldom practised, the mere threat of it being sufficient to keep a wife on her good behavior.

This doctrine of Woman the Pursuer, reaching back to Spenser's Britomart and antedating Shaw's Ann Whitefield Tanner, Lytton represents as a deliberate Vrilya policy. Women, they say, are not only more intellectual than men but more affectionate, and more exclusive and stable in their emotions. Their reasoning is that "unless the Gy can secure the An of her choice, and the one whom she would not select out of the whole world becomes her mate, she is not only less happy than she otherwise would be, but she is not so good a being, that her qualities of heart are not sufficiently developed; whereas the An is a creature that less lastingly concentrates his affections on one object; that if he cannot get the Gy whom he prefers he easily reconciles himself to another Gy; and, finally, that at the worst, if he is loved and taken care of, it is less necessary to the welfare of his existence that he should love as well as be loved."

This situation is illustrated by the episode of Zee falling in love with the inferior human, or Tish, who had dropped into their world from the outer crust of the globe. She had already made three journeys alone into distant provinces in search of a lovable An but with no effect on her heart. Her unfortunate choice is thus commented upon by her father, Aph-Lin: "It is, as you imply, not uncommon for an unwedded Gy to conceive tastes as to the object she covets which appear whimsical to others; but there is no power to compel a young Gy to any course opposed to that which she chooses to pursue. All we can do is to reason with her, and experience tells us that the whole College of Sages would find it vain to reason with a Gy in a matter that concerns her choice in love. Zee, as a Gy, cannot be controlled; but you, as a Tish, can be destroyed. I advise you, then, to resist her addresses; to tell her plainly that you can never return her love. If you yield, you will become a cinder." Thus admonished, the intruding, inferior, English Tish resisted the importunate Zee, and was, by her generous assistance, aided to return safely to his native haunts on earth's upper crust.

The purest matriarchal type is shown in Hudson's dream of a Crystal Age wherein everything centers around the mother-worship of the secluded and enthroned matron head of the family. This is the full flowering of the tiny feministic bud glimpsed in Bacon's seventeenth century New Atlantis; at the lavish annual Feast of the Vine when the clan celebrates its prolific human garner with bountiful elegance, father presides at the head of the table, but mother attends by occupying a lofty traverse above the right hand of the patriarch, behind "a carved window of glass, leaded with gold and blue; where she sitteth but is not seen."

The superiority of Woman is announced also by Delisle Hay's Voice from Posterity; and she dominates likewise on the French Îles Bienheureuses, on the German Insel der Grossen Mutter, and on Mars as seen by Henry Gaston. This last locality sets the new style in companionate marriage. The first union is an inconspicuous affair with divorce ready on demand, but at the advent of the first child the parents are remarried publicly, permanently, and with great éclat. These ratifying weddings occur in batches, a dozen at a time, amid high rejoicing and with the babies as guests of honor.

In Timothy Savage's Amazonian Republic an old tradition is utopianized. The lost ex-midshipman wandering about in Peru is captured by cannibals on the way from Lima, but has the luck to be recaptured by a scouting party of feminine warriors. This transfer proves to be a rescue and the captive becomes a trophy. He is conducted by his kind captors, valiant and beautiful as Walkyrie, to their magnificent semicircular city, where the government is conducted with great dignity and efficiency by gracious ladies in charming costumes. The men are correspondingly feminized but seem resigned to their passive rôle.

Of the purest matriarchal type is the small secluded Empire of the Nairs, as reported to us by James Lawrence early in the nineteenth century. This community over in Malabar abolishes marriage and exalts maternity. The men are chosen by the women as lovers but ignored as fathers. The children belong entirely to the mothers. When young boys are in need of good manly counsel or assistance they look to their maternal uncles, who stand in loco patris, and are in a manner the guardians of the clans. The government provides an ample subsidy for mothers, on the ground that women should be well paid for their production and care of humanity's most valuable asset, the perpetuation of the race. Every increase in the family brings a corresponding increase in the salary. These women are not, however, Amazonian in their rule. The joint crown rests on the Samorina and whatever Samorin happens to be her brother, son, or nearest male relative on the maternal side. Life is so free and easy that it calls for little work or responsibility, but the men are saved from becoming effeminate by being bold and dashing warriors. And quite appropriately, since the fighter must have somebody to fight, the spirited and high vocation of the masculine population is waging war against the Mohammedans, those wicked brutes who enslave their women.

The realm that out-feminises feminism is another underground North Polar region called Mizora, where man himself is abolished and a colony of lovely majestic and intelligent blondes have lived for centuries by achieving human parthenogenesis. They dwell in houses of elastic glass, communicate by radio, travel in air-ships, are nourished by chemical food, and invoke the laboratory instead of

Jupiter Pluvius when the country needs rain. They have attained to moral heights by eliminating the inferior. The last, and now historic, criminal was a woman who once struck a child.

Even this airy leap of the fancy is out-vaulted in Shaw's *Back to Methuselah*, which goes farther forward than backward, and tells how in the year 31,920 the adolescent human will be hatched from a mammoth egg. In an earlier and more realistic portion of this drama, but still in the future tense, occurs the incident of Zoo, the beautiful benignant woman who specializes in children because she is the born mother.

In Maitland's *By and By* unmarried women are paid by the State for the adoption of children if they desire the maternal life without marriage. Charlotte Haldane's *Man's World* is another instance of vocational motherhood; only the superior women are permitted the honor of bearing children, but the "neuters" may engage in any career, including that of licensed courtesan on the old classic model. Mantegazza pictures his Paul and Marie journeying in the year 3000 from Rome to the World Capitol at Andropoli to secure from the Biological Senate permission for parentage. On the way they pass through the Islands of Experiments, among which are Poligama and Poliandra. They are granted the privilege they seek, and (not an irrelevant fact) Paul wins the prize for his invention of the psychoscope, an instrument for reading other people's thoughts.

By the year 6922 feminism has reached such an extreme, according to Maderiaga's *Sacred Giraffe,* that a counter-reformation is started in the African center of civilization. The radical reactionaries have rough sledding because the feministic road has been smoothed by the snows of countless yesteryears. Hominism is repulsed by the conservatives as being a thing unheard-of, unnatural, and therefore immoral.

From these numerous Utopian facets we get their separate rays of light rather than a blended shaft. Some retain marriage but belittle the home. Others are all for the home but would free it from marriage. Some are sure we are lost unless we preserve both. Others exultantly throw both into the same discard. Some subordinate the Home to the State. Others would rate all other institutions as means, and only the home as an end in itself. Yet even these last fail to paint any very alluring picture of the hearth or boudoir. Their Lares and Penates are enshrined images that never come to life.

Since maladies of every kind are banished from Utopia, or reduced to a minimum, it could not be expected to harbor homesickness, any more than other ills. But this particular misery might absent itself for a different reason. For after all the sincere and intelligent Utopian effort to solve the domestic problem, the Utopian home emerges as an establishment which would not induce by reason of absence from it any severe case of nostalgia.

CHAPTER IX

THE SATIRIC SUBURB

THERE is nothing of which the human race is more fond than of humor and mirth; nothing to which it is more prone than censure and criticism. When rebuke takes the form of ridicule it becomes satire. And nowhere is the satiric attitude more prevalent and freely expressed than in and around the world idealized. Satire on Utopia is met by the retort of Satire in Utopia. Satire in Utopia extends all the way from occasional quips and taunts to being the main substance. These latter performances are caricatures made more dramatic by masquerading as highly approved portraits. Sometimes the reprimands they convey are too bitter and earnest to come under the heading of satire, but such of them as are here mentioned are included as pertinent criticisms. For rebuke is, after all, the matter of satire, and ridicule only the manner.

What draws the satiric dart is of course simply the opposition. The object satirized represents in every case the satirist's innate and temperamental dislike. Utopians are by no means immune from the ubiquitous virus of antipathy. Each one is constrained to build his own little millennium, from whose vantage point he spits fire at the antagonistic millennia and at the unregenerate actual world that is so smugly satisfied with its own disgraceful failure. Whereupon the smarting world retaliates by making unmerciful fun of the quack's absurd nostrum for the incurable disease of mortality.

As for finding those two apparent contrasts, the scoffer and the perfectionist, rolled up into one, that no more than indicates the reverse sides of the same thing, for idealism is but the silver lining to satire's frowning cloud. By a fit coincidence, the first Utopian is the best example of this combination. Sir Thomas was burning with indignation at the social stupidity and political knavery that were ruining his beloved England. But most of his disgust was vented on the way, in the quiet deadly irony of the long avenue of approach to his constructive picture. His distant Athenian predecessor was also impelled by discouragement with his present, but Plato could placidly dissect the body politic to search for obscure embedded justice, dealing his suave strokes of mockery as by-play, whereas More could be mildly mischievous in Amaurot only because he had exposed the sad truth in Antwerp.

Johann Andreae had more of a caustic vein than might seem native to a grave Lutheran pedagogue. He comments dryly on "the handsome logic" of a government that consistently makes bad matters worse. He sends a few random shafts at strutting councilors, "sucking the sap out of others' goods and fattening lazily"; also at lawyers, doctors, the worldly clergy, the idle rich, and the officious wives who "keep giving their husbands advice, and never in season." He remarks acidly that in Christianopolis the teachers are not "men from the dregs of human society nor such as are useless for other occupations." And he deftly puts his finger on the vital spot by adding that those citizens are too wise to "expose the very valuable, supple and active youth to the vilest, most vicious, insipid and coarsest men, merely because such may be had more cheaply." This Utopian has no illusions about the race of mortals,—"so deep are the secrets of the human heart, so generous our rating of ourselves, so bold our critical judgment of others, so subtle the apologies for human errors." He counts it fair game for the satirist: "The world has faith in the unbelieving, follows the blind, is mortally afraid of the weak, raises the lazy, and admits heaven knows what absurdities. It ought not, then, to take offense when some one laughs at it."

For the most part those who view with amusement as well as alarm express their views in the inverted Utopia whose purpose is to exhibit our civilization to itself by implying the discrepancy between the ideal and the real, as well as that between the real and the supposed, that yawning gulf which separates what we are from what we think we are. The same "good ship Phantasie" that conducted the German theologian Andreae across the Ethiopian Sea of Stupidity to the Island of Peace in quest of Wisdom, steered the English Bishop Hall to his "World Other yet Same." This proves to be the Glutton's Paradise, a Land of Cockaigne where we meet the feeders as well as the food (the corpulent ancestors of Morrison Swift's Horroboos), who make edibles the medium of exchange, and worship the god Time who devours everything. A thriving city of this realm is Garrula, a feministic province is Viriginia, and a neighboring territory is Moronia or Fooldom.

A more general travesty is Jonathan Swift's Eden of Houyhnhnms, where he shows by means of horses, as Aristophanes had shown long before by means of birds, how preposterous it is of the human creature to speak of "the lower animals." And a more specific one is Lord Erskine's Armata, the true Mundus Alter et Idem. He tells of the ship Columbia, whose exploring crew, roaming the South Seas, are caught in a mystic stream bounded by high stone walls. For three months the vessel is carried along the rushing current and finally beached on a planet which proves to be earth's twin, connected with it by this double channel seventy thousand miles long. The sole survivor is rescued by a brother Englishman who years ago had been stranded there in the same fashion. Everything he says about this country called Armata, its capital Swaloal, its neighbors Patricia and Capetia, its distant daughter Hesperia, constitutes an ironic judgment on England, Ireland, France, America, and British affairs generally by the look-on-this-picture-and-then-on-that method. Similar treatments of the same subject are seen in Mangin's *Utopia Found,* Disraeli's *Captain Popanella,* and McCrib's Scotch *Kennaquahair.*

An anonymous skit in the eighteenth century uses the future vision to satirize the contemporaneous George III by picturing the success of his descendant in the twentieth century as *The Reign of George VI.* This latter-day George rules from 1900 to 1925. Although of a pacific disposition, the king is a great hero in the wars with Russia and France, and is ultimately crowned Emperor of France, Spain, Mexico, and the Philippines. In his own country the national debt is reduced, science and art encouraged, and magnificent public buildings constructed. We are told that in 1920 the United States have a population of eleven millions and are prospering under the British rule that they never had thought of repudiating.

Later in the century the slightly allegorical and satirical Travels of Hildebrand Bowman, Esq., into the provinces of New Zealand labelled Carnovirria, Tanpiniera, Olfactaria, and Auditante, on to the Island of Bonhommica, and through the powerful kingdom of Luxo-volupto in Australia, are in the vein of Bishop Hall's *Mundus Alter et Idem.*

In the nineteenth century John Minter Morgan gives us a more carefully worked out symbolism in his *Revolt of the Bees*. This describes in pungent detail the pernicious effects of the propaganda which turned the happy communal hives into disastrous competitive individualism. The scene is laid in the apiary of Logan House at Pentland Hills, Scotland. The leading bee citizens are Elia, Orpheus, and Emilius. Through their little drama wealth and poverty are revealed as the morbid symptoms of a diseased body politic. One incident shows a poor plaintiff waylaid by a lawyer as he is hurrying to court in search of justice, and relieved of all his honey for a retaining fee. In contrast to the ensuing gloomy Trial is placed the frivolous Butterflies' Ball. While the industrious but defrauded insects are floundering in their predicament, the spirit of Allan Ramsay appears to them and points out that their suffering was caused by the folly of abandoning their cooperative instinct and clumsily imitating man at his own elementary stage, before his reason had matured. As an object lesson he unrolls before them a prophetic vision of humanity a century later when cooperation has brought about a millennium among mortals. Instructed and heartened by this prospect, the chastened bees return to their original system.

In the meantime the Danish Professor, Ludvig Holberg, narrates the adventures of Niels Klim, who falls through a cave in Norway and lands upon a grotesque but highly civilized territory governed by a regal paternalism. Debates are forbidden but new projects may be submitted and are given a fair trial. If successful, their proponents are heroes; if failures, their advocates are classed as criminals for raising false hopes and wasting time. Niels himself is banished back to the upper crust (their severest punishment) for proposing to disfranchise the women. Among their laws, one exempts all parents from taxation; and another forbids anyone under thirty to write a book.

Among the moderns Archibald Marshall uses the same device of falling through the earth and landing in an ostensible Utopia, the Upsidonia where wealth is disgraceful, poverty exalted, and all hands zealously are playing the great national game of Giveaway.

Quite unattuned to this note of rollicking mirth is the caustic tone of Anthony Trollope's *The Fixed Period*, a story which grimly ridicules the notion of settling on a definite year for shoving superannuated citizens off the map. The tale is told in retrospect by the former President of Britannula, a South Sea colony that had swarmed over from New Zealand. We gather that this tenacious fanatic, Mr. Neverbend, had become head of the government and dominated the legislature enough to push through a policy that was an obsession with him. This was the gentle shoving out of existence by the euthanasian route all citizens who had crossed the threshold into old age. By such a prompt and kindly act all the evils and expenses of a prolonged doddering senility would be avoided, to the benefit of the community and its encumbrances alike. To establish the location of this threshold was a matter of some difficulty, but after a long congressional dispute it was placed at sixty-seven and a half years. On his sixty-seventh birthday each one in turn was to be conducted with great pomp and honor to the College, a charming Old Folks' Home, where he was to spend his last months in luxury and indulgence, and sometime before his next birthday to be painlessly snuffed out. The first test case is made of Gabriel Casweller, hale and hearty at sixty-six, still productive and efficient, far more fit to live than to die. What with a romance between his daughter and Neverbend's son, complicated by a visit of the British Cricketeers on a sport tour, and other episodes, the story of how the tyrant was foiled and deposed invests the satire with considerable excitement. More interesting, however, than the ironic fantasy itself is the fact that it was written when the author was sixty-seven, that it was the last year of his life (by fate's decree) and that enough of the remarkable Trollope vigor was left to produce in those few months two serial stories and two other volumes besides this lively protest against premature death.

In confining his satire to a single issue and that a rather personal one, Anthony Trollope stands at the extreme of concentration. At the extreme of diffusion is the impartially eclectic ridicule in Moszkowski's *Isles of Wisdom*. We might imagine that the sixteenth century Brandt-Barclay Ship of Fools had sailed down the stream of time with its German-English cargo and come to port in the twentieth century Russian archipelago, which happened to be situated in Bacon's New Atlantis locality. For this Northern Pacific harbor is hospitable to every variety of stupidity and fanaticism. Vleha Island is the Eden for Epicureans. Baleuto is Plato's Republic materialized as a freak. Kradak, the Isle of Perversions, shows why genius is allied to insanity. Sarragalla, the Mechanized Isle, is the apotheosis of efficiency, especially in the time-saving department. And the utter futility of saving time is shown in Varreia, the Reactionary Isle. In Heliconda we see esthetics gone mad and all feeling sublimated into the one sense of smell. Obalsa is the Isle of Hypothesis, where everything acts as if the false were true. There are also the Isles of Relativity, of Skepticism, of Pacifism, in this variegated assemblage.

This system of assorted ideals has counterparts in the more serious pictures by Magnus and Mante-

THE SATIRIC SUBURB

gazza, and the more mordant by Sweven and Ollivant. The latter's *Tomorrow* is a genuine Utopia with satiric by-play through the character of Jax. This creature was originally a normal youth who had a fancy for studying and reproducing the past, —that is to say, our present. He began as an investigator in Zed's Experimental Station but soon became so influenced by this past that he took on its character. Caught in its environment as in a trap he was irresistibly propelled backward through the centuries. He had thus rolled down hill until he was recognized as on a par with the nineteenth century, a hideous degenerate, absurdly decked with clothing, salacious, greedy, filthy, and pious. Among his decent contemporaries he was an atavistic freak, but over on the Islands he was at home with his own kind. For, like Sweven's Limanorans, these futuristic people had banished their Diehards after the great reformation, and now their relics, including the lawyers and clergymen, were living the vulgar competitive life in safe isolation with their antiquated barbaric theory and practice.

The most complete and adequate example of the inverted Utopia, with its covert irony turning a dry devastating light on a whole civilization, is Samuel Butler's *Erewhon*. This hidden paradise, tucked away "Over the Range" in New Zealand, is an Upsidonia that is logically Rightsidupia. From its consistent people we get the disconcerting effect of seeing our pretty theories put into actual practice. We are forced to admit that as a triumphant inescapable exposure this picture takes the prize. In the real world, for instance, we pretend to regard illness and incompetence as misfortunes but we penalize them as though they were crimes. In Erewhon they are openly admitted and treated as such. Their law courts find the sick defendant guilty of consumption, for naturally a man has no right to be disabled and incapable of supporting his family. A culprit convicted of being swindled is heavily fined, since it is illegal to be a gullible dupe of clever sharpers. And just as disease is a crime, so is crime a disease, calling for appropriate therapeutics. No upright citizen would confess to having a cold, but the most virtuous might boast a bit of his bad temper or parade his kleptomania, in order to get sympathy and condolence. The two main bulwarks of their sound sturdy conservatism are the Colleges of Unreason, which expertly smother common sense and independence, and inculcate the diplomacy of sitting on the fence; and the Musical Banks, which purvey a soul-satisfying religion of esthetic sentiment without reference to tiresome and inconvenient ethics.

A much more sardonic gibe over our basic incapacity to be civilized is Halévy's terrible story, *Four Years*. (A part of the volume *Luttes et Problèmes*). It seems that in 1925 Ziegler's Concentrated

Food had done away with toil and pauperism, but at the price of an excessive leisure that bred an orgy of insanity and suicide. By 1950 things are at such a pass that everybody welcomes the next invention, Novgorod's Drug, a compound which permits the pathologic victims of their own folly to conclude a fifty-hour debauch with an ecstatic death. At this mad juncture a saving remnant of scientists and saints, quenching their natural mutual antagonism in their common desire for a normal healthy life, work valiantly to stem the tide; but they so arouse the hostility of the suspicious populace that in 1973 they are disqualified from holding public office. In 1997 degenerate Europe falls an easy prey to a terrific epidemic that purges the country of several worthless millions and also sobers the mob enough to bring about a temporary acceptance of discipline and reason. But as soon as the panic is over, the old incorrigible distrust, jealousy, prejudice, stubbornness, revive the old innate antipathy, and the final destruction is at hand. This day of retribution is saved at the eleventh hour by the only force powerful enough to induce cooperative effort. That force is no less than almighty War, a Horseman of the Apocalypse who comes galloping out of the East. The Orient is mobilizing against the Occident, but the embattled enemy is Europe's deliverer, for it is a human enemy, a target of our own flesh and blood and therefore an appealing focus for the venting of energy, a gloriously fightable adversary. A thrilling scene is staged in Paris as one by one, Italy first, Holland last, the desperate countries fall into line and vote for Union and Combat. With zealous efficiency Militarism soon has the defensive organization complete except for the small item of a rousing International Hymn. Fervent collaboration, however, presently produces this inspiring slogan:

> More hate, more wars, more captives and jails!
> All men are brothers and their love never fails!

It happens that four of the Utopians have written companion pieces, the satiric picture in every case preceding the idealistic. The ensemble chances also to have a cosmopolitan quartering. The French skeptic who exclaimed, "How dismal will be the perfect state of society for which we sigh!" and yet could not resist contributing his own sample, offset his *White Stone* by his *Penguin Island,* an Aristophanic bird-fable wherein we are invited to admire their State "firmly based on the two great virtues: respect for the rich and contempt for the poor."

The English priest achieves a sharp religious antithesis that might be labelled Night and Morning. Benson's *Lord of the World* is a gloomy forecast of the catastrophe inevitable if the Protestant forces instead of the Catholic get into the saddle. By 1914 socialism is established with general massacre of all opponents. By 1917 England is communistic, under the leadership of Oliver Brand, presented in all fairness as a man of sincere and magnetic personality. Julian Felsenburg, the World President, is an American of tremendous ability and fine character. The government is smooth and efficient. Its laboratories dispense practical information. Its compulsory education, regulated inheritance, old-age pensions, prison reform, aim at justice. The use of Esperanto facilitates racial harmony. There is luxurious housing with all ingenious scientific devices, much of it underground, in a calm and quiet region perfectly lighted and ventilated. There is much air-travel by swift volors. Humanitarianism is exalted into a State Church, with a picturesque symbolic ritual on the Masonic model.

This sounds like an authentic Utopia, but with all his conscientious giving the devil his due, Benson sees this situation as essentially devilish because the material progress entailed spiritual dissolution. Oliver Brand's wife, a lovely and noble woman, is driven to end her life in the government House of Refuge, after the eight days of reflection required by the Release Act. His aged saintly mother returns to the Roman fold on her death-bed. Rome itself along with its Holy Church is ruthlessly and utterly exterminated. From the Catholic point of view the cataclysm is complete.

From its ashes arises the Phoenix *Dawn of All*. In this rosy dream, disturbed only by a few satiric mutterings, Benson is ravished by the sight of all Christendom, now enlarged to include practically the whole globe, united under an Emperor-Pope. Church and State are again one, the latter subordinated as wife to husband but restored to monarchic prestige. The Bourbons are recalled to adorn the French throne. Italy is an Austrian vassal. Mexico and South America are parts of the great Spanish Empire. The Pacific Coast of North America is conquered and colonized by Japan, but the remainder of the United States is joined to Canada as an English, and orthodox, province. The Orient is under Papal arbitration. The Irish have been transported to Australia, and Ireland converted into a huge monastic retreat and a sanatorium for all psychopathic patients; these are pronounced cured when they display a total self-suppression and submission to authority. Westminster is once more a Benedictine possession.

In this ecclesiastical universe political suffrage is granted to about one in seventy, and business is carried on by guilds (as in Morris's future London) with the several trades and professions distinguished by costumes and vivified by gorgeous ceremonies. The irreclaimable socialists and infidels have been transported from their last stronghold in Germany to an assigned district in Massachusetts, where they are permitted to purge themselves of the poison of democracy or to die as hard as they please. The new civilization has abolished divorce and established heresy courts. These are justified through the poignant episode of Dom Adrian Bennett, a Benedictine Monk and Doctor of Science, who passionately affirms his loyalty and denies that he is a heretic, yet argues that if the Church thinks he is, he should be executed. It does and he is.

Such transient shadows, however, only intensify the permanent radiance. Society is "no republican stew-pot in which everything tastes alike," yet its return to medievalism does not exclude the appropriation of modern inventions. Dictographs and radios are commonplaces. The magic volses, in which you embark after being shot up to their lofty station-platforms by air pressure in hollow tubes, are everyman's vehicle. The story comes to a magnificent climax in a world gathering to celebrate the stupendous Catholic victory. The envoys arrive from all points of the compass, and their mammoth air-fleets, converging into a splendid colorful joyous pageant, remain poised in the heavens while the vast multitude swells the jubilant chorus of a very heaven on earth.

The wise Scottish Sweven, quite as ardent an idealist, is much more of a satirist. He has sufficient mordant wit to construct an entire Archipelago of Exiles (akin to the "Isles of Wisdom"), and to in vest in addition his Island of Progress with the gleaming aurora australis of lambent irony. Riallero was the dumping-ground of those obstacles to advancement extruded from the aspiring Limanora. Here they settled down and kept peace among themselves by allowing each of the numerous islets to specialize in its own brand of silliness or villainy. Tirralaria becomes the harbor of socialism, where the tourist's guide, Garrulesi, waxes eloquent over its advantages, oblivious to its lethargy, stupidity, and squalor; but in his temporary absence these are exposed by the renegade Sneakape, who demonstrates how this regime rests on slavery of the cruellest sort, since a "liberal" government means freedom to discipline the workers. Vulpia is the nest for politicians, whose most astute device is drafting their worst nuisances into the editorial or clerical profession, where their loquacity can have an innocuous outlet. Criminals with the usual turn for piety are given the option of a life sentence to prison or a career as priest or journalist. The only drawback to this scheme of providing a safety-valve for bubbling oratory was the protest of the Church's soundest sleepers who had fitted up their pews as dormitories and objected to being kept awake. The bright idea of another group that promised well was an automatic listener, more important than the mechanical speaker, as it gave people relief from paying attention along with uninterrupted indulgence in talking. Unfortunately it failed in plausibility because it could not register the suppressed despair of the buttonholed sufferer, his irritable attempts at interjection, his pathetic efforts to escape. The Limanorans themselves had discovered loquacity to be a germ disease, and cured patients who were bursting with the obvious and babbling as if their views were of importance, by skilful surgery and inoculation.

The American novelist Howells imports his Traveller from Altruria and reverses the usual procedure by having the visitor observe our mundane affairs from a Utopian background instead of the other way around. The mysterious Mr. Aristides Homos is a guest of Mr. Twelvemough and a student of the renowned American Democracy. His ingenuously consistent behavior and his artlessly embarrassing questions create an uneasy excitement among the complacent Bostonians elegantly rusticating at a fashionable summer hotel. When their inconsistencies are innocently exposed they bristle like defensive hedgehogs. The inquiring visitant is finally made to understand the snobbish preacher, the hardboiled financier, even the tired business man, better than the busy and exhausted society woman, who squanders her energy until she is a nervous wreck merely for the sake of killing time. Mrs. Makely, the exemplar of this curious use of leisure, also defends social caste by the same infallible reasoning. The poor, she contends, must exist in order to enlarge the sympathies of the rich, yet the rich must refrain from yielding to their sympathetic impulses, because charity pauperizes the already indigent. She can elucidate fluently why the sight of an idle tramp is debasing and the sight of an idle plutocrat inspiring. In the sequel, her friend Mrs. Bellington Strange marries Mr. Homos and migrates to his Altrurian home, whence she writes to Mrs. Makely an account of their idyllic life in that southern isle. Her letters constitute the second part of *The Eye of the Needle,* the first half being a continuation of the caustic *A Traveller from Altruria.*

Utopia itself is satirized as far back as *The Anatomy of Melancholy,* wherein Burton's Democritus, expanding the "merry fooling" of Shakespeare's Gonzalo, imagines the sport in cleaning up the world with a high hand. He will make his own New Atlantis where he can freely domineer. It will be on an unknown Australis or Floating Island or in middle America or northern Asia. There he will have a stern but kindly monarchy, and make faces at Plato, Andreae, Campanella, and the whole communistic outfit. The eighteenth century produced two anonymous French burlesques, *La Nouvelle Cyropedie,* and *L'Île de Naudely,* the latter apparently ridiculing Fénelon's *Télémaque.* In the nineteenth century Mallock's *New Republic* implies amusement at the entire perfectionist project. Mark Twain contributes his skeptical bit by his conclusion that "where there is no fever of speculation, no inflamed desire for sudden wealth, where the poor are all simple minded and contented, and the rich are all honest and generous, where society is in a condition of primitive purity, and politics is the occupation of only the capable and patriotic," there is a Utopia in the literal sense of being Nowhere.

This ironic pessimism as to the possibility of reaching an ideal goal is out-Heroded by Aldous Huxley's mordant denial of the existence or desirability of the goal itself; a view covertly but clearly avowed in his just hatched *Brave New World*. His brilliant travesty is in the vein of Butler's *Erewhon* and Zamiatin's *We* in its cool inflexible propulsion of a syllogism along the path of Logical Conclusion to the terminal of Reductio ad Absurdum. Push the present tendency, he implies, to its extremity of realization, and what have you? You have the eternal paradox of perfection: that you don't want what you want, and can't have what you must have.

In Huxley's future London, evidently in the twenty-sixth century, as the date is After Ford 632, the T Model Civilization is established and running things according to the Utilitarian Gospel. The greatest good to the greatest number is achieved by a universal though graded diffusion and enjoyment of the major materials of happiness: robust health, adequate training, congenial and moderate work under pleasant auspices, ample and varied provision for recreation and entertainment, communal outlet for religious emotion (in the Ford Singery), elimination of the need for ethics, guaranteed security, absence of all friction, and finally a quick transit from the full tide of activity to a luxurious euthanasian exit, impeded by no traffic with illness or senility.

This miracle is accomplished by beginning at the beginning. For the now obsolete and disgraceful viviparous birth is substituted an artificial incubation expertly manipulated. The pre-natal influence is carefully calculated to prepare the members of the coming generation for their respective destinies. Future residents in the tropics, for example, are so treated while still in the embryo bottle as not only to endure heat but to prefer it; while prospective aviators are accustomed to precarious balance and unstable equilibrium.

Temperament and disposition are thus already fixed when the baby is decanted, but the fixing process is rigorously continued by the social pre-destination nurses. Infants meant to be common laborers are inoculated with a distaste for books and flowers by being made to associate these innately attractive objects with harmless but terrifying electric shocks.

THE SATIRIC SUBURB

Since an efficient civilization requires five classes of citizens, from the lowest operative I.Q. to the highest practical intelligence, this T Model has provided the correct proportion of Alphas, Betas, Gammas, Deltas, and Epsilons, each shaded into pluses and minuses. And since this efficiency also demands a vast majority of the lower orders, the proper ratio is secured by the Bodanovsky method of proliferating the three under castes in great quantities at the expense of quality. This is done by a system of embryonic pruning and stunting that grows duplicates, running as high as ninety-six identical twins from one stock. These masses, from the moronic Epsilons to the mediocre Gammas, form the triumphant solution to the previously insoluble problem of how to get the world's work done without some sort of compromise. The very need for compromise is deftly nipped in the bud by this elemental shaping so that each and every citizen actually likes to do what he has to do and is smugly satisfied with his lot, whatever it may be.

This policy was luckily reinforced by the accidental discovery of the useful hypnopaedic device. (In an incident which refers to GBS as one of the very few whose writings are still extant.) While real knowledge cannot be imparted in this way, the plan is invaluable for the instilling of formative precepts. Under each pillow in the children's dormitories is a radio which whispers soft persuasive reiterations of appropriate sentiments. Into all sleeping Gamma ears, for instance, is poured the sweet refrain, "I'm so glad I'm a Gamma," with enumeration of the Gamma privileges and the disadvantages in all other grades.

While the Alphas and Betas are permitted to develop a normal individuality, they too are brought up on slogans which officiate as motivating reasons: "Never put off till tomorrow the fun you can have today;" "When the individual feels, the community reels;" "Everyone belongs to everyone else." "Spending is better than mending." This last is an encouragement to extravagance in order to keep consumption up to production, production itself being less of an economic necessity than a psychologic. The working day is kept at approximately eight hours mainly for the curtailment of a superfluous and potentially dangerous idleness.

The moderate amount of leisure is doubly safeguarded by plenty of sliding-scale amusements, from athletic sports to social diversions. Even journalism is neatly adapted to its readers; publishing *The Delta Mirror* in words of one syllable, the sensational *Gamma Gazette,* and an *Hourly Radio* for Alphas and Betas.

And if any of these should pall, or life unaccountably go flat and stale, there is immediate relief in soma, a potent but innocuous drug always available. Incipient symptoms of restlessness or de-

THE SATIRIC SUBURB

pression are promptly checked by remembering that "A gramme is better than a damn." It is an office of friendship to whisk a companion out of the blues by quoting "One cubic centimeter cures ten gloomy sentiments," or "A gramme in time saves nine."

Upon a normal inhabitant of this brave new world nothing ever would pall. But since it is its creator's intent to exploit all its mechanical perfection as a sharp foil to its vital imperfection, he must introduce the critical and rebellious element to lodge the complaint. This he embodies in a trio of recalcitrants. Foremost is Bernard Marx, whose freakish atavistic behavior would make him a baffling puzzle were his associates not able to account for him on the theory that too much alcohol got spilled into his blood surrogate, thus locating an Alpha plus brain in a Gamma minus body.

> (And so the conditioning didn't take,
> Making his life one long mistake.
> What, then, did the hand of the bottler shake?)

The unhappy Bernard is mildly abetted by Helmholtz Watson, Professor of Emotional Engineering, that is, composer and teacher of feely scenarios and hypnopaedic maxims, who is stifled by the consciousness of his own suppressed power and originality. And later both are reinforced by John Savage, who represents the alien and unreconciled import. When these three precipitate a crisis and are haled before the Great Mogul who holds the reins of this beneficent but strict autocracy, the ensuing frank discussion crystallizes the philosophy underlying the whole tale.

The sympathetic but inflexible Mustapha Mond has to remind his young insurgents that even Utopia is subject to the laws of cause and effect, of sacrifice, and compensation. The best population, he observes, is like an iceberg: eight-ninths of it below the water line and better off than the one-ninth above. He concludes that since all these fractious objectors are clamoring for is the right to be unhappy and the freedom to be square pegs in round holes, there is nothing for it but to let them blow off their own steam, far enough removed, to be sure, from the world they repudiate to keep it safe from their contamination.

In this expedient of preserving harmony by muting the discord, the author follows the beaten Utopian track. Indeed, except for his very ingenious dramatization of the latest scientific findings and trends, Mr. Huxley is no more original in the portrait he paints than in the significance he attaches to it. He echoes Lytton in Watson's discovery that chronic satisfaction is death to art: "You've got to be hurt and upset;" he exclaims, "otherwise you can't think of the really good, penetrating, x-rayish phrases." And in Mond's assertion that "nobility and heroism are symptoms of political inefficiency," the efficient regime leaving no scope for high altruistic impulses, he says amen to Wells. Neither did Huxley invent the reversed morality that regards a permanent, possessive, and exclusive affection as unseemly and indecent, and an impartial promiscuity as your only true and virtuous respectability. More startling than his innovations is the tacit suspicion they arouse in us that they are not so novel after all. Has not mortal man always been conditioned by his heredity and shaped by his environment? Is he not educated by dogmatic precepts, impelled by winds of doctrine, cowed by tribal taboos, passive, plastic, and predictable? Human circumstance, in this dashing burlesque, has the charm of the unreal; human nature has the charm of the familiar.

Being a satirist, Mr. Huxley is obliged to amuse. Most of his comic effects he gets from his wicked fooling with Ford. His pages are well peppered with the patter of the day: "Ford alone knows;" "Ford bless you;" "His Fordship;" "Ford's in his flivver; all's right with the world." But under this surface facetiousness lurks the caustic wit of a soul in a sad panic over melancholy prospects.

In his lively interest in science and his unquenchable zest for its incredible performances, Aldous is not Huxley for nothing. But in his sentimental prejudice against materialism, his romantic antipathy to mechanism, he does seem to be a Huxley for worse than nothing. If his prancing imagination were curbed with more of the family common sense and a real sense of humor, it would be less likely to shy at Utopia as a dreadful bogey. A similar discipline would improve the pace of his logic. It is easier to announce than to prove that "Mass production demands the shift from beauty and truth to comfort and happiness." The use of that last word in fact betrays a lapse into the prevalent hedonistic fallacy,—an incomplete and nebulous definition of terms. It is also easier to declare than to demonstrate that comfortable circumstances are incompatible with kinetic characters. Huxley's thesis seems to be that a thorough and continual gratification of the sensuous desires is possible but only at the price of all spiritual aspiration. The truth of that depends entirely upon the human side of the equation. Esthetic and intellectual opportunities always have been utterly wasted on people whose outfitting stopped with the physical and emotional endowments, and always will be. Those who are gifted with minds and souls, so far from letting them perish will rather use them and whatever ministers to them. Practical intelligence arranges for adaptation to environment. Sagacious wisdom modifies and to a degree creates its own environment. Huxley does not make it perfectly clear why he feels it necessary to rule from his brave new world all the highest

THE SATIRIC SUBURB

human faculties. But the fact that they are ruled out is precisely what injects sarcasm into the title, and makes his Utopia a burlesque instead of an ideal.

Aldous might indeed con to advantage the recent utterance of his brother Julian, a statement running true to both Huxley and Arnold form in its illuminating diagnosis and prescription:

> No community has ever yet set itself seriously to the task of scientific humanism. No nation has really attempted to think out what are the valuable things in life and the relations between them, or to work out the best means of realizing these values in fullest intensity and proper relative dosage. A few individual thinkers have tried their hands, but until society as a whole gets busy with the problem, individual attempts will have little effect.

This is a call for all idealists to perpetuate the precedent set long ago by Sir Thomas More, pioneer Humanist and Utopian, and to continue that happy fusion until humanity becomes scientifically Utopia-minded, and its Utopias become increasingly humanistic.

His story is really an illustration of the pronouncement made by another dubious critic, who opines that what man wants is "not a Utopianized Chatauqua but a peace full of virile and adventurous satisfactions." But Mr. Wiggam has led his phrase in backward. What he meant was a Chatauquanized Utopia. It is just such muddle-mindedness as this that has provoked such retorts as John Ruskin's "Utopianism is one of the devil's pet words;" and Jack London's corollary, "Anything can be damned by calling it Utopian."

Thus what with the pessimists jeering at the optimists, the idealists fleering at the cynics, the Utopians themselves flouting one another, there has been no lack of thrust, parry, and counter attack, with no immediate prospect of a truce.

One object of satiric assault indeed has had so much attention that its story is reserved for special consideration. This is the form of government. All Utopians bank confidently on environment and its power over supple human nature. This environment is largely formed by the type of public policy. Moreover, since government is man-made, flexible, amenable to improvement and decidedly in need of it, it forms a bright focus for satire, an alluring target at once abstract and concrete. But while the debaters agree on the importance of good government, they are at fighting odds over what kind is good.

The following section will give some account of the immemorial rivals, conservative and radical, particularly as represented by a buzzing and stinging swarm of refutations and repudiations that flew out angrily from the conservative hive and did battle with a dangerous radical intruder who threatened the safety of the established camp.

CHAPTER X

VERSUS BELLAMY ET AL

THE challenging figure who raised the mightiest disturbance, both pro and con, in all Utopiadom was by no means the original communist; but he was the first to dramatize his views so effectively as to become a best-seller long before such broadcasting was the commonplace it is now. The circulation of Edward Bellamy's *Looking Backward* and the number of languages into which it was translated would make stupendous statistics at the present time, and the more astounding nearly forty-five years ago.

Yet the reasons for this wide-spread and vigorous reaction are evident enough. The book appeared at a moment when the air was full of troublesome theories just percolating into the popular consciousness, and the public was feeling the need, in its vague way, of a clarifying catalysis. When this was offered in the form of a spirited absorbing story, furnished with real live characters, elaborated into a comprehensive program of daily living in all its homely details, animated by a passionate sincerity, persuasive without dogmatism and earnest without solemnity, it was irresistible. And the more it succeeded as propaganda the more it had to be attacked and confuted by the opposition.

Not the least of Bellamy's assets was the pungent satire with which he drove home his points. His metaphoric stage-coach, drawn by human power, was later borrowed by Jack London for his *Iron Heel,* with the amendment that the aristocratic riders are as tightly chained to the vehicle as are the proletarian pullers. His ramshackle tenement carefully preserved as an object lesson of the old regime grew into the Museum of Ancient Horrors featured by most of the subsequent Utopias, with special attention paid to the Nineteenth Century Room. Another jab at that ludicrous competitive era is made through a picture in the new Boston Art Gallery. The painting shows a crowd of people in a rain, each man holding an umbrella over himself and his wife, and giving his neighbors the drippings. To a populace that took the adjustable municipal awning-umbrella for granted this scene appeared as a telling satire on that extravagant and uncomfortable time. The satiric climax of the book comes in the penultimate episode—Julian West's dream of awakening back in 1887, going through the routine he used to accept as a matter of course but now through his enlightening blissful experience viewing it as a dreadful and intolerable situation, culminating in the disastrous dinner party on

Commonwealth Avenue. It is the second and ultimate awakening in the year 2000 and the joyful discovery that the other was the dream and this the permanent reality, that gives point to the happy ending.

Of this tale's numerous aftermaths four were in the nature of reinforcing sequels: the author's own postscript, *Equality*, Geiseler's *Looking Beyond*, Schindler's *Young West*, and Stroebel's *Die Erste Milliarde der Zweiten Billion*.

In Geiseler's applausive echo the main incident is a debate between Professor Forest (a character borrowed from one of the adverse retorts, Michaelis's *Looking Forward*) and Mr. Yale, a Bellamite, wherein the latter does his cause proud and wins the honors. The story concludes with a Limanoran sort of inter-stellar outlook. Communication with Mars has been established, and the new Earthian harmony utilized to further the great planetary intercourse. All the cohesive human energy formerly generated only by threat of war (as in Halévy's *Quatre Ans*) is now aroused by the shame of provincial ignorance; and this combined fear and pride are fused into an ambition for cosmic knowledge and for a creditable position in the Federated Universe.

Schindler's contribution is in the shape of an autobiographical sketch made by Julian West's posthumous son, known even in his old age as "Young

West." His story is a testimony to the perfection of his environment. From the beginning in the delightful nursery-school, through the grades and the public college, he is affectionately scrutinized for signs of special talent, and every aptitude discovered is carefully fostered. This is no concession to his personal position but the typical treatment. Boy scouts and youthful sponsors aid in self-government. When on the grand annual festival of Muster Day the young people enter the Industrial Army as the middle-aged retire, there is no conflict over vocation or precedence. With never a dissenting voice nor a discordant note, every citizen sees his duty and does it. Young West himself advances from post to post until he attains the final distinction of becoming Commander in Chief of the Army and thereby President of the United States. The narrative ends with a rather wistful exposure of his father's private journal, a document which is indeed quite in accord with Julian's public utterances but which confesses a keen personal unhappiness in an alien world to which no one could become so suddenly acclimated.

Stroebel's offering comes late enough to be one of the recent post-war reactions. His looking backward is to the year 1930, the date when the New Society celebrated the first decade of its progress. The reformation had started in Germany in 1920, and spread rapidly both east and west into a successful realization of Bellamy's Utopia.

But over against these few commending supports stand a dozen or so scandalized protests designed to refute Bellamy and the Bellamites and to counteract their deadly influence.

The first voice to be lifted, and that promptly in 1890, was Vinton's, whose *Looking Further Backward* presents Professor Won Lung Li, successor to Professor Julian West at Shawmut College. His lectures on American History form the substance of the book. Not as an exchange professor, cultivating international amity, does the Oriental occupy this Occidental Chair, but as a member of the race then dominant in America. The Chinese are in this pleasant position because their country alone kept her head when the rest of the world was swept off its feet by the cyclone of Socialism. Conquest of such a demoralized globe was easy. In the year 2020 China had declared war against the United States on the ground that it was a defensive measure necessary to combat the American Red Peril in the Orient. Confronted by a military crisis, our socialistic President could only appoint a committee to remonstrate with the invaders, and this moral suasion somehow missed fire. The trespassers were not interested in logic, nor even rhetoric.

After their victory the Chinese employed the old

Babylonian method of exchanging populations by deportation and colonizing. The course of the conflict is traced through the fortunes of the West family, who tried to escape on a hand-car and in freight trains, but encountered everywhere the helplessness of a mechanized routine in the face of a real emergency. Julian was killed in the battle of Erie, leaving an unpublished journal much more candid and critical than his official report. His son, young Leete West, was adopted into the new regime and made an officer in the local militia. It is interesting to note that the oriental part of this story is antedated by P. W. Dooner's *Last Days of the Republic,* which was published in 1880 and gave a lurid picture of the conquest early in the twentieth century of the United States by China.

Vinton's ominous warning was followed the very next year, 1891, by four more, all made in Germany,—besides the American *Looking Beyond* already mentioned.

Richter's *Zukunftbilder* was aimed directly at his own countryman, Bebel, and is given a plausible air by the reasonable tone of the narrator, Herr Schmidt, who keeps a journal during Germany's little flier in Communism. The successive entries reveal the slow puzzled painful course of this ardent but honest radical as his glowing confidence paled to doubt, and doubt finally yielded to dismay when the failure of the great experiment became too patent for any denial.

For Wilbrandt's book the trans-Atlantic stimulus is indicated by the title. *Mr. East's Experiences in Mr. Bellamy's World* expresses some dubiety about Mr. West's experiences, and criticizes his version of them with mild shrewdness and grave courtesy. Mr. East relates how in 2001 Socialism had converted Berlin as well as Boston, but not into a paradise. All the evil results—lowered production, inefficient mass management, resentment of personal interference—soon bring about such a catastrophe that the leading characters flee the accursed spot (as in Richter's tale) and leave the tangle to unkink itself as best it can. Bellamy's mouthpiece, Dr. Leete, is explained as a credulous old dear whom everybody ridicules behind his unsuspecting back.

The title of Mueller's volume also carries its own reference: *Ein Rückblick aus dem Jahre 2037 auf das Jahr 2000. Aus den Erinnerungen des Herrn Julian West.* The book achieved three editions in its first year, the third displaying the medals it had already won in compliments:

"Sincerely recommended to all of Bellamy's readers who have allowed themselves to be deceived by the sophistries of the fluent American."

"This little book presents a welcome supplement to Bellamy's superficial but dazzling air-castle."

"One does well to pursue here the further adventures of Julian West."

It is supposedly Julian West himself who, after a frank and apologetic Preface, proceeds with his supplementary and disillusioned story. The rift in the lute starts with the appearance one morning in the Professor's office at Shawmut College of a young worker with a troublesome problem. This was a matter of family feud. The youth's father, an able and responsible physician, had been urged under strong pressure to give an official bill of ill health to a certain young Whitford, whereby he might dodge the dangerous position to which he had just been appointed on a flood-relief commission. Dr. Norbert's refusal prevented this evasion of duty but unfortunately the youth died in the performance of it, and for this the Whitford clan had taken a drastic revenge on the physician. They had enough prestige and influence to demolish his practice and force his son into the vocational side of schooling, thus cutting this youth off from the history he was so anxious to study. As a typical circumstance this incident leads to a long impassioned revelation of the constant graft and reprisal going on under the government's unsniffing nose. West's natural sympathy with this case and his tactful efforts to right the injustice bring him too under the ban as a vicious reactionary.

Hounded down by the loyal Press, West loses his

Shawmut position and goes to Washington to appeal to the President. General Harcourt proves to be a modern Cromwell, righteously despotic. He was prepared for his visitor and promptly explained to him that his unpopularity was due not only to his suspicious interest in Thomas Norbert but to the tone of his lectures on the French Revolution. Now these had really been quite literal and sincere, but the sharp mistrustful public had interpreted them as a sly ironic parallel to the present American condition. The President admits the tyrannic rule and confesses also that he deceives the people by masking his own hard-headed realism under the approved idealistic gloss. He was aware that the original strike was not for freedom but for bread. Well, now the people had their bread and circuses to boot, with no call to demand freedom. As for the economic equality guaranteed by the credit cards, one was obliged to wink at the fraud and intimidation constantly practised, as long as it was done under cover and not found out.

West's own dilemma is solved by the compromise of another job in return for his open support of the President's policies. He is appointed sheriff of a small western town, whither he repairs and sends for Edith. But his wife calmly refuses to leave Boston, where she is busy being Supervisor of a Municipal Breakfast Room, Secretary for a Women's Library, and Patroness of three Girls'

Schools. She does, however, consent to join her husband at the charming southern villa of the Chucklebys, where they have been invited to spend a fortnight.

The genial reactionary, Mr. Chuckleby, serves for Mueller's spokesman, for Julian's eye-opener, and for esthetic vestigial remains of the old regime. He lives in Harmony Castle on a plantation leased from the State, and to his guest's freshly perturbed spirit this easy, ample, solid home, with the fields full of happy laborers and the house manned by satisfied servants, is an individualistic oasis in the vast communal desert. It is, moreover, most sweetly adorned by the daughter, Floretta, who is a nineteenth century enthusiast and makes an eloquent plea for its restoration. Mr. Chuckleby enjoys his special dispensation the more, as no others had any choice of residence or locality. Recently an edict had been passed forbidding emigration from Louisiana, a practical provision, for "who would not rather live in healthy California than that pestilence-ridden district?"

This delightful sojourn over, Julian West proceeds to Ebertytown, and comes upon a parlous state of affairs. The new sheriff tries his best to be a new broom, but the brisker his sweeping the thicker the dust. He is further hindered by the two people from whom he had expected help. One is Thomas Norbert, now half crazed by his misfortunes and stumping the country as a ranting radical. The other is Edith, who decided to come, after all, but found the contrast between this boorish provincial village and her cultured and convenient home city too great to be endured. While the storm of their personal miseries is threatening to break, the sudden death of President Harcourt precipitates the brewing anarchy. The final upshot is that Edith marries Thomas Norbert, Julian is released to wed the more congenial Floretta Chuckleby, and the whole chastened country returns to the capitalistic system, modified by a state ownership of all the land.

Quite as dramatic a political protestant as Ernst Mueller, with the added fervor of a religious crusade, is Philipp Wasserburg. Under the pseudonym of Philipp Laicus he wrote his *Etwas Später!* in a highly exclamatory state subdued to a tone of patient devotion to truth. His subtitle is *Eine Fortsetzung von Bellamy's Rückblick aus dem Jahre 2000*, and his preface explains that this sequel is situated in an orthodox and monarchical environment in order to exhibit the difficulties not inherent in Bellamy's America. Cuba is therefore chosen as the field for an extension of the communistic propaganda. It seems that about 1950 the island had been freed from Spain and annexed to the United States. At first the inhabitants were pleased with the change but soon realized that the American ideal of enterprise and energy and commercial skill put too great a strain upon people of indolent temperament, in an enervating climate, accustomed to slave labor and an idle aristocracy; so that their plight was worse than before. After much investigation and consultation things were still at a discouraging pass in 2000. Then someone had the bright idea that Julian West would be the very one to send down there as a soothing emissary, his mission being to persuade the reactionary Cubans that the good old times they were sighing for were really not so good as they fancied. Having lived in them, he should know.

Julian is willing enough to undertake this errand, but is decidedly dashed to find that Edith cannot accompany him until she is through with school, and need not even then unless she wishes to. For this version of the story has Miss Leete married at twenty, with a year of compulsory education ahead of her. (Dr. Mueller's version also stresses the point that Bellamy's boasted free college training for all merely operated to keep the stupid and indifferent expensively marking time, and remarks that in Ebertytown many of the students were already spouses and parents.) After a long and heated powwow it is decided that they will defer the trip until Edith graduates, and that she is to enroll for her novitiate service in Cuba, remaining there for that three year period.

Finally arrived in Havana the Wests are appalled at the disreputable condition of the city, in a state of medieval squalor. And just as they reach their own unkempt dwelling they are outraged by the spectacle of a woman being bound to a post and given a lash by another woman in uniform. At her shriek Julian rushes to the rescue with horrified protest, but is assured there is no occasion for alarm, as at the first stroke Estrella had promised to work. If she kept her promise, not another blow would fall. She was one of the Spanish patricians who would lie around on the sofa and smoke cigarettes all day unless compelled to perform their small stunts.

The feministic side of socialism, woman's equality in freedom and responsibility, is the hardest thing for the chivalric West to swallow. When his wife decides to enter the hospital as a nurse, and calmly ignores his violent objections to that arduous occupation, counters his arguments, and smiles at his threats of prohibition, he broods sadly over a marital order that so undermines conjugal authority. Another source of friction is their different religious attitudes. Julian was conforming to his traditional creed in a somewhat vague and thoughtless manner while Edith was an ardent and conscientious atheist. Among their acquaintances they happen to number three German Jesuits who are on tour studying American schools. Edith not only out-argues her husband but carries the battle into the enemies' camp. Of course she ultimately falls under the spell of the irresistible priests, and her final surrender is the more impressive because of the terrific struggle preceding the overthrow of her staunch scientific skepticism. The Catholic victory acquires great prestige through the intelligence and logical acumen, the earnest sincere character of its ransomed soul. Having become converted Edith is as vigorous in her adopted belief as are all proselytes. The Wests, now ecstatic over their release from socialistic shackles, decide to return with the Jesuits and live in Germany, which now has the truly ideal regime.

The story of this Teutonic Utopia is told to the new adherents by Father Neumann. It began with a war between France and Germany in 1940, followed by such a welter of disorder that finally out of the muddle evolved a common consent to accept Catholicism and entrust all sovereign power to the Papacy. The previous communistic abolishment of religion and marriage had roused all good citizens to rally round the slogan, For God and Our Children! A Council of Five now constitutes the governing body and extends its sway over secular education. The State owns all the land, guarantees work for everybody, and requires uniform costumes.

Julian and Edith are not only admitted to this Eden but are subsidized by the United States as envoys and student-guests. On their arrival at Hamburg they find that America is threatened by invasion from Russia via Siberia. Like Mr. Vinton, Herr Wasserburg is impressed with the defenseless position of a socialistic state when exposed to foreign attack. He turns danger into a happy ending, however, by invoking the aid of other foreign powers, instead of permitting a natural destiny to take its own course. Although these powers do not approve of America's present policy, they assume it to be a temporary madness from which she will be purged by this peril; and in any case Russia must be balked of her ambition. So the story ends in the thrilling commotion of all Europe mobilizing to save this misguided but valuable America from Slavic spoiliation. As counter propaganda it bears the marks of its canny Jesuit authorship, and belongs with Benson's *Lord of the World* as a prophetic warning in which politics is secondary to religion.

The next year, 1892, saw the anti activities cut in half. And of its two volumes, only one is a direct retort to Bellamy. The other, the lurid *Caesar's Column*, by the Ignatius Donnelly of Bacon-Shakespeare notoriety, repeats Wasserburg's method of glimpsing a real Utopia in conclusion, thus heightening by a final shaft of radiance the gloom of the main story. The scene of Donnelly's Reign of Terror is in a future New York, where the surface of life is made perfect by marvellous mechanical appliances, and the daily routine smoothed and systematized by the puissant machine of communism. Underneath, however, run the deadly plottings of rebellion, headed by the Dark Brotherhood. When these boil over and spread a horrible ruin over the fair landscape, the two families who survive fly by airplane to a safe refuge in Africa. Here snugly ensconced in Uganda (neighbors unaware to Hertzka's Freelanders) the fugitives settle and flourish under a system that features education both free and compulsory, inclusive literate suffrage, minimum wage, restricted fortunes, and a soviet legislature elected by groups of workers, merchants, and artists.

The year's other offering, openly anti-Bellamite, was *Looking Forward*, by Richard Michaelis. This time the narrative is continued by Julian West himself. One morning as he enters his history class at Shawmut he observes a stranger of somber aspect sitting in the back row. This proves to be Professor Forest, former incumbent and West's predecessor, but now deposed to a janitorship as penalty for his reactionary teachings. So outraged were his contemporaries by his respectful attitude towards the past, by his defense of the competitive and capitalistic nineteenth century, that they would have committed him to an insane asylum but for Dr. Leete's plea for tolerance and a less drastic punishment. The doctor himself is interpreted as an able politician, upright enough but not above using a pull or accepting a plum; also as something of a practical joker. Forest proceeds to unmask the present situation. The farmers are feeling abused and discouraged. The statesmen are torn between the conservatives who rebel against favoritism and injustice, and the radicals who clamor for a sweeping abolition of religion, marriage, and regulated incomes. Everything is so bad it is bound to be worse.

Michaelis hints at his own Utopia, defining it as a cooperative industry in guild form, with a graded income tax, limit of inheritance to a quarter of a million, limit of land ownership to forty acres, government ownership of public utilities, and a national bureau of statistics to supervise and control production.

In 1893 the list is augmented by Fayette Giles's *Shadows Before,* which tries to throw an extra shade on Bellamy; and *Looking Within,* by J. W. Roberts, carrying the sub-title, "The Misleading Tendencies of *Looking Backward* Made Manifest." To Mr. Roberts the story of Julian West was no less than a basilisk, an upas tree, a fog, and a bane which poisoned multitudes who never saw it first hand but caught the germ as one does during a deadly epidemic. As an antidote he prescribed the story of James North. This young man and his betrothed, Effie Solon, through a series of accidents and coincidences, awaken in 1927 from a trance of thirty-five years. They find the United States in the throes of a labor and capital war, and the crisis so desperate that, although happily married in 1928, they cannot live happily or usefully in a chaotic world. They decide therefore to take another Rip Van Winkle nap, this time for seventy years, from 1930 to the end of the century. When their automatic arousal occurs they find themselves in a land apparently calm and prosperous, but to them a strange and lonely place. Hearing that there is another stray soul in the same predicament, they journey to Boston and receive a warm welcome from their contemporary Julian West. For in spite of their differing viewpoints, these relics of the past century enjoy their common bond and mutual reminiscences.

The Norths are also delighted with Dr. Leete but not impressed with his philosophy. They diagnose him as a sentimental optimist, so wrapped up in his ideas and so pleased with the fair surface of things that he does not see beneath it. It is from the Chief of Police that they learn what is really going on, a depressing and horrifying revelation. Mr. Hume opens their eyes to a city underworld of vulgarity and crime. Turning for relief to the country they encounter Mr. Acre, who informs them that the farmers are furious and about to start a revolt in their own idyllic fields.

Two years of this are all the Norths can stand and they agree on a respite of twenty-five years in oblivion. Recalled from this in 2027, they find things at last looking up. America has learned its lesson and has returned to individualism, retaining the practical items from the abandoned experiment.

The year 1894 was another prolific season, yielding not only *Young West* and *A Traveller from Altruria,* but a critical-reconstructive tale, *The English Revolution,* by Henry Lazarus, and Frank Rosewater's *'96, a Romance of Utopia.* There is more romancing in this last than Utopianizing, but it is made dramatic by the always effective device of antithesis, a double portrait of failure and success.

After the usual fantastic preliminaries the characters in this tale find themselves in a deep mountain-rimmed African valley, the crystal Land of Lukka, where everything used is some form of glass and nature has an entirely novel color scheme. The Lilliputian inhabitants dwell in two cities, the circular Tsor in the east and the rectangular Tismoul in the west. Tsor is the bad example, old and sunk in iniquitous dotage. Like Campanella's Sun City, the metropolis is centered about the temple of the state religion. This dominating structure, Kar Yuk, is a gigantic pyramid encircled by terraced flights whose outer walls are decorated with historical and scientific paintings. But here the presiding deity is Zmun the God of Gold. The inner surrounding circuit or First Avenue is called Kar Yim and composed of palaces and mansions. Tok Yim, on the outer circumference, is the business and manufacturing district. Before the doors of these last buildings are platforms continually crowded with kneeling suppliants for admission. Those who cannot contrive to get in are haled off to Kar Tuki, the black crystal prison and poorhouse. The whole place is seething with restless misery kept only by force from breaking out. Presently the force proves weaker than the pressure against it, and its hell breaks loose.

The good example is Tismoul, which in the meantime has been taking lessons by telepathy from American Democracy; not, be it understood, the traditional spurious brand, but the genuine article, installed in 1896, as a guild-soviet with suffrage limited to the intelligent and educated. By 1930 the entire western hemisphere had been organized into one harmonious State, and the eastern was in line for federation. Tismoul is thus in high feather, with her cooperative cuisines, her community clubs and libraries, her public dining halls where private rooms may be reserved for families, her farmers living in social centers and motoring out to their fields for work, her housewives paid for domesticity as a standard profession, her children granted a regular subsidy while going to school. It is her industrial rivalry that plays havoc with Tsor's unstable economic system, and precipitates the eruption and holocaust. Whereupon the friendly competitor Tismoul, now rechristened Utopia, sends a relief army to succor and instruct, and in the end the two are merged into a happy union under the modern enlightened plan.

And so the good *fin de siecle* work goes on. When the complete history of this decade is told, now being so zestfully exploited as "mauve" or "yellow" or "gay" or "romantic," one small item should not be omitted,—that in the period from 1891 to 1901 no fewer than forty of these Utopian plants sprouted, and a few of them bore fruit both edible and nutritious.

The four decades that have elapsed since *Looking Backward* inspired so many lookings in every direction have produced results of a sort at the rate of two a year, although not at regular semi-annual intervals. So far the twentieth century has grown more satire by the reactionaries than by the radicals. Down on the subterranean Lost Atlantis a "Scarlet Empire" holds sway by the familiar formula of sodden drudgery, short rations, unflagging espionage, and brutal punishment. Rebels are fed to the behemoth Kraken. The imperilled visitor is saved from its greedy maw by a timely volcanic upheaval which casts him back on earth, where he blossoms into a moral plutocrat, his socialistic taint being thoroughly washed away in the salt flood.

Barry Pain's "New Gulliver," shipwrecked on Ultima Thule, discovers a race burrowed in just beneath the surface. As the boomerang of a communistic orgy, a handful of crafty intellectuals now holds in subjection a horde of menials, granting them just enough comfort to keep them in prime working condition. Like the Vrilya, the aristocrats have a death-dealing rod which they use freely on the lazy and disobedient. This perpetual sitting on the lid has its penalty for the sitters. Printing has to be excluded in order to keep learning a secret. As a birthday gift, the Professor of Old World History places at the Central Office an order for his friend, MZO4, Controller of Light and Heat, the precious privilege of reading a manuscript.

In the year 2020 England is in the clutches of Horace Newte's "Master Beast," alias Socialism, and the monster is raging and devouring in a fine frenzy. But the perennially youthful stranger, asleep this time since 1911, together with the great-grand-daughter of the girl he was engaged to marry back in the good old days, contrives to elude his brutal jaws and to assist in muzzling them.

Meanwhile Jack London's "Iron Heel," alias

Capitalism, is enacting the tyrannic rôle over in America. Ultimately the crusher is crushed and the happy era of the Brotherhood of Man inaugurated. In 1932 Mrs. Everhard writes an account of the struggle up to 1917 and hides the copy in a hollow oak, where it is found seven centuries later, 419 B.O.M., and published by Anthony Meredith, who continues the narrative through its brighter stages.

The only Utopian to be ridiculed as openly as Bellamy was Blatchford, whose *Sorcery Shop* was burlesqued by Herbert's *Newaera*. Although this story slumps into absurdity in the end, it starts out in a judicious and constructive manner. Young Frank Ledingham is bequeathed by his wealthy father the whole island of St. Michael wherein to put his socialistic theories to the test under the most auspicious circumstances. He is to have a lavishly complete equipment and a selected personnel of colonists. There are to be ten thousand of these pioneers, all professed socialists but with a previous record of economic success,—no scum and dregs. Frank's first blow is the refusal of the prominent crusading socialists to join the enterprise. This disillusionment is followed by others in rapid succession. He thought he had guarded against this by "not setting up one of the usual socialistic Utopias, where all the women are beautiful, all the men athletic, all the thorn-bushes always covered with peach-blossoms, and where the people do nothing but talk capitalism all day long;" but he found reality less plastic than fancy. He is driven to ask plaintively: "I have read many descriptions of socialistic societies, but there never seemed to be the least difficulty, nor any need of discipline or control; the people all worked, and worked well, because they liked it. Why can't ours do the same?" And finally, confessing failure and escaping by stratagem, he returns to England highly resolving to devote the rest of his life to counteracting the effect of his baleful venture.

By another accidental dualism the fore and aft of political theory are given a piquant contrast on the same stage as to time and place. The Germany of 1970 is the scene of Pezet's *Aristokia*, where socialism is playfully bantered, and of Gregory's *Meccania*, where imperialism is shown up with a caustic touch.

Pezet explains that when the world goes into a state of Universal Democracy in 1930 it is indulgent enough to reserve a section for the immutable aristocrats, where they might dwell in exclusive isolation. This patrician minority is deported to Prussia, by the way, about the time the socialist minority of the *Dawn of All* is deported from it to New England. Admission to Aristokia is made through the Board of Royal Blues, and the little colony, where of course nobody works, is amply financed by an annual summer tourist season. It becomes the world's playground because the world's dutiful workers flock for their vacation to the one spot where they may drink, gamble, and gaze at snobdom in its native haunts. To the visitors this "deliciously quaint world of marriages, divorces, scandals, and duels," is a grateful change from their clanging machinery and ugly environment. More than that, however, it affords opportunity for the higher recreation of drama, music, art; the proletarian order having expelled the dreamers and thinkers along with the drones and parasites.

Meanwhile Gregory's Chinese Mandarin Ming is travelling through Meccania the Super State, personally attended by Sheep, Sub-Conductor of Foreign Observers, and examined by Stiff, Inspector of Foreigners. Everyone must keep an official diary, and if his day shows more than one hour unoccupied, the Time Department assigns some cultural pursuit and sees that it is pursued. Family expense budgets are supervised, and all purchases made from samples on view in each ward, as in Bellamy's Boston. Amusements are free, on the bread-and-circus policy, and the educational drama compulsory, for it presents made-to-order plays on such instructive themes as Efficiency, Obedience, and the Futility of Democracy. The people are divided into seven classes, distinguished by the color of their uniforms, and the number in each class kept fixed by the Births Department. There is an annual Strenuous Month which not only gets a lot of work done but induces a becoming sense of relief and gratitude for the months not so strenuous.

Back in 1888, coincident with Edward Bellamy's *Looking Backward,* Walter Besant's *The Inner House* made an earlier display of the seamy side of communism. It heads the line of gruesome tales but has a unique fantastic plot. According to this invention, a tremendous furore was created in London in 1890 by Professor Schwarzbaum's public announcement of his discovery of an elixir capable of prolonging life indefinitely. As a result, we are introduced to this same generation still living centuries later but in a state of arrested development, crushed under a despotism in communistic guise. The dictator is a ruthless vulgar egoist who holds the fort with the aid of his selected henchmen. In all this time there has been but one death—by accident, of course—and one prearranged birth, to keep the population static. This new member of the community, a young woman of intelligence and imagination, is appointed Curator of the Museum of Antiquities, and through familiarity with these quaint relics becomes enamored of the past, like Mueller's Floretta Chuckleby. Christine also has initiative and proceeds to play a daring game. She selects a few of the stultified, torpid, apathetic creatures whom she knew by the records to have belonged to the old aristocracy, and induces them to spend a few evenings playing at dressing up in the old costumes and dancing to the old music. In spite of their inertia they are gradually seduced back into the old atmosphere until their dormant recollections are awakened, stifled romances bloom again, and they are enchanted at this dramatic revival of themselves as individuals. This group then plans a revolution, is captured by the alarmed authorities, is about to be executed, is saved at the last moment, turns the tables on the tyrants, blots out this evil experiment like a bad dream.

Twenty years later in his *Republic of the Southern Cross* (translated from Russian to German by Hans von Guenther) Bruzov says a similar thing in a more mocking voice, though his persiflage deepens into a tragic instead of a happy ending. The center of world civilization is now at the South Pole, where another great circular city has been established by three hundred steel workers. This metropolis is entirely glassed in and over, heated by electricity, and connected with the distant towns and villages by covered passages. The fifty million inhabitants are prosperous under an autocratic communism. Government provides education, entertainment, recreation, medical and legal service, and religion of all brands, together with a generous pension after twenty years of active work. People so well treated should be able to put up with a censored press, uniform dress, and an early curfew for everybody. Their contentment was first ruffled, however, by a mysterious epidemic called Widerspruch. For a score of years it was merely sporadic but by and by it spread and grew beyond all bounds and control. Psychiatrists made a special study of this Mania Contradiceus and found the disease impelled its victims to do or say the opposite to anything and everything mentioned or suggested. At first the symptoms were rather comic. Car conductors refused to accept fares and insisted on paying the passengers. Visitors to art galleries rehung all the pictures up side down. But at last the endless and universal disputing and quarrelling became so serious that the badgered citizens were going daft and committing suicide wholesale. The best neuropathologists were baffled and the community became one vast raging madhouse. Finally the sane remnant were rescued by airplanes and conveyed to the old erratic but endurable world.

Condé Pallen calls his *Crucible Island* "a Romance, an Adventure and an Experiment," but it is only another revamping of the worn old theme. On an island east of the Bermudas is a settlement organized by socialists deported from other countries by international agreement. The latest arrival is Carl Runder, a German communistic firebrand sentenced to the Spielgarten of Schlechtland. He is conducted, blindfolded and manacled, up a mountain, unbound, released, and told to march on alone down the road ahead. To falter or look back means instant death. Scared out of his wits he runs till he drops exhausted and faints. On recovering he finds himself on a lonely trail but just above a beautiful valley that unrolls an alluring panorama before his astonished eyes. To his utter amazement and delight he learns that this sunny peaceful retreat is not only lovely to view but supplied with ample resources for easy and comfortable living; not only that but, rapture's crown of rapture, it is inhabited by kindred souls, his own fellow-socialists who had this congenial haven already prepared for him.

For a month or so it is as if he really had died and gone to heaven. Then the paradise subsided into a purgatory whose slack vacuous tone grated on the newcomer's dynamic spirit and checked his soaring idealism. The people were industrious enough; they held themselves to a six-day week, with a three-day vacation every three months. But they had no ambition beyond their routine labor and trivial diversions. The next drop was into a blasting hell of tyranny. Carl had fallen in love with the one maiden in the valley possessed of beauty, grace, warmth, and mentality. But marriage and home were discarded barbarisms, matches were made by the Council of Welfare, the assigned couples were paired off at an annual ceremony on a two-year contract, and parents never even saw their own children. All this was brought home to young Runder when he saw his cherished rosebud, Mina Clausen, rudely picked by Herr Schmidt, Head of the Council and a most obnoxious and repulsive Uriah Heep. And there was no chance of escape, for while these radical repudiators were allowed to live after their chosen fashion, they were not allowed to change their residence even after they changed their minds. It was a life sentence, with positively no parole nor commutation. However, after a desperate struggle and stratagem Carl and Mina, together with her father and their friend McCarthy, slip out of the cruel crucible and over to America.

The latest of these derisive sneers is by way of rebellion against the most startling of modern experiments. Zamiatin's *We* is an exhibition of Sovietism firmly mounted and prodding with silent spurs. In Russia's far future there is no longer You or I, He or She. In a beautiful city of magnificent, symmetric, transparent buildings the inhabitants go about in their light blue unifs performing their designated tasks with rhythmic precision. They attend in a body their public entertainments, which are agreeably spiced with ridicule of the old haphazard chaotic regime. The first sign of mutiny is nipped in the bud by a surgical operation which removes the last shred of personality and turns the dangerous citizen into a placid and useful Robot. The story is told through the diary of D-503, builder of the interstellar airship designed to transport to other planets a share of the "mathematically faultless happiness" achieved on this. In many ways this satire is an inverted *Limanora*, one of them being its organic nature, so infused by the mood and style that no transcript of it can be given by synopsis or excerpts.

All this Utopian tartness gets its tang, acidulous or acrid, from the partisan flavor. Yet this very antagonism is neutralized by the fundamental identity of the complaints. What every critic objects to is the hypocritical ruthlessness of the party in power; always, strangely enough, the party he does not belong to. When the communist protests against the iron heel of the minority, and when the individualist resents the strong arm of the majority, each one is sure he is exposing the tyrannic wolf masquerading as the beneficent sheep. And whenever it is true that the people, like Morrison Swift's African Rinyos, merely exchange one despotism for another, each denouncer of oppression and subjection is so far justified.

In the satiric parade just reviewed the partisanship is all on one side,—naturally, since the company is composed of defenders of the established individualistic order against the hostile socialistic usurpation. It does seem to be the case that the embattled defense devotes itself mainly to brandishing the satiric sword, while the forward striving offense flashes it only as an incidental weapon. The reason for this is evident enough in the basic difference in their situations. As always, the conservative has nothing to do but protect and preserve, the more passive performance of the besieged. He has therefore the more time and ammunition available for checking the opposition. But the radical has on his hands not only the preliminary job of demolition; he is responsible also for the reconstruction. He is accordingly too busy with his double enterprise and too seriously concerned for its success to afford more than a by-play of ridicule for the stubborn hulking obstacles in the path of his advance.

The thing to remember is that these mutual enemies are but human; and while the great heart of humanity is usually in the right place, not so much can be said for its head. And yet, since it is often from the clash of such half truths that the whole truth first manages to emerge, this warfare is not without some significance and value.

CHAPTER XI

THE WORLDS OF H. G. WELLS

In all this discussion of the Utopian solar system no mention has been made of the worlds contributed by Mr. Wells. The reason for this omission is, of course, not his negligible status but his exceptional importance in the realm of constructive idealism. He is the creator of an entire universe, and although his planets have their several places in the total scheme, they form enough of a cosmos to be segregated for the moment and considered by themselves.

There are about a dozen of these creations, sent spinning out at intervals during a third of a century, and located all along the cosmic radius from the inner zone to beyond the periphery. Nor have we any reason to suppose that the author's exuberant productivity is ended. His latest Utopia may not be his last. Yet all this is one branch only of his versatile performances. His collection of polemic but realistic novels bulks even larger. But he has a fondness for romance, combined with a penchant for speculative prediction, and vitalized by his steadfast ardent belief that human progress is not only painfully necessary but actually possible. This fusion of basic traits spells his manifest destiny as a specialist in Utopias.

Mr. Wells began with a trio of fantasies, products of last century and his own experimental stage. His *Story of the Time to Come* projects us into the twenty-second century, amid the terrible efficiency of a scientific materialism. There is neither home nor country life. The radio has put reading and writing out of business. Rapid transit has made walking a lost art. The urbanites ride around the streets on their circulating sidewalk, equipped with seats and built at different levels, each more speedy than the one below, to a maximum of fifty miles an hour. Out in the country they glide in electric motors over rubber pavement, at twice that rate and more. Yet Mr. Wells absent-mindedly allows the nineteenth century to adorn this advanced period with such charming little anachronisms as bicycles, and tall betrimmed hats worn by ladies even in the theater.

In his *When the Sleeper Wakes* this preliminary sketch is expanded into a full design. When Graham comes out of his trance into the same time, place, and circumstances, he finds all industry in the hands of the same Universal Labor Company, only it is more of a beneficent octopus than ever. It guarantees employment to all who apply, but naturally it assigns the work and pays the minimum living wage. The incompetent who cannot rise above the serf class are born in the Company's crèche and die in its hospital. It has abolished pauperism but has put more than a third of the population into its blue canvas uniform. These costumes are made wholesale while you hardly wait, and the public diversions (furnished and encouraged over the distrusted acquirement of learning and culture) are on a similar huge scale. Parents spend the evenings at the phonograph-dictograph-spectroscope or at the merry dances while the children sleep peacefully in the Company's nursery. The other two-thirds, however, are bored by their leisure and patronize the Euthanasy Syndicate as a means of evading old age and shortening life's inanity. Dying under its auspices is expensive but handsomely done.

The Time Machine introduces us to a totally different scene and atmosphere, yet its situation is but these others pushed to their logical conclusion. The inventor of this magic lightning express makes a little jaunt to the year 802,701 and back again between lunch and dinner. As proofs of his breathtaking excursion he brings back a few scratches and scars, torn and disheveled clothing, and a ghastly tale of this farthest future. He had landed in a lovely sylvan spot and encountered a race of exquisite fragile creatures, as colorful, sportive, and indolent as butterflies, at once artless and artistic, yet with all their childlike merriment evidently under the spell of a vague and sinister dread. Not for economic efficiency do they spread their dainty tables in a large refectory and assemble in a common dormitory for sleep, but from a constant haunting fear which seeks safety and reassurance in companionship. They are terrified, the visitor soon learns, of the Morlocks, a ghoulish underground tribe, bleached, red-eyed, simian, who are invisible by day but slink around furtively at night, preying upon their victims. It then appears that these beings are really slaves whose subterranean status evolved inevitably from the mines and subways of the preceding eras. By this time they are in sufficient subjection to be forced to do all the work and to be kept out of sight, but they wreak their revenge by waging ceaseless, covert, malign warfare against the beautiful but weak masters whom they are gradually destroying. The whole picture is a symbolic impressionism on the theme that a tightly wound tyranny may whirl for long and long on its own momentum but is bound ultimately to run down and topple over or to be tripped up and thrown away.

These initial exploits of Wells do not, however, set the pace for his later Utopian feats. On the contrary, he seems to get the Jeremiah out of his system by these youthful deliverances and thereafter becomes more of a Deutero-Isaiah; like him and the other Hebrew patriots in making his prophecies of the joys to come "in that day" emphatically conditioned on our own actions rather than proclamations of destined certainties.

The World Set Free is, for instance, a prediction of the mighty effects of radium. It is the most dramatic of the forecasts of which Wells is so prolific, and a typical example of his habitual instantaneous application of scientific discovery to everyday life. Any news from the laboratory is to him an intoxicating mental stimulant which operates through his alert imagination to practical ends. In this tale the release of atomic energy is presented as accomplished in 1933 and utilized by 1953 through the Holsten-Roberts Engine. This machine necessitates the scrapping of coal, oil, steam, steel, and other previous agencies of material progress. A scientific revolution coming too suddenly and on too sweeping a scale is bound to precipitate a social chaos. Out of this must be wrought a new cosmos but it will demand the utmost resources of human intelligence and energy. The World War in the middle of the twentieth century is a symptom of such readjustment; and the World Republic which finally emerges from the struggle is a monument to our reconstructing power.

In the Days of the Comet and *The Dream* are miniature idealisms set in wide romantic frames. In the first we are told how the entire globe is enveloped in a green gas caused by a comet which just grazes it in passing. For the space of three hours all life is suspended. But when creation breathes again it does so with a new ease and freedom, for the meteoric atmosphere has swept along with it all the baleful influences in our own. Mankind awakes to a fresh purified environment where sympathy and tolerance prevail, concessions are made, even to the sharing of family ties, and individual homes are merged into a beauteous community.

In the second we are introduced to a lad of the lower middle class, and are made to perceive through his heroic but thwarted striving for an education the barbarous nature of a "civilization" so cluttered up with obstacles to any desire for improvement. Against this foil shines his dream of the true culture that succeeds the fortunate destruction of the old and spurious. The vision is of the idyllic order, verging on anarchy, and looks more like a Morris landscape than one by Wells.

More Wellsian in every respect are the two that are the most concentratedly Utopian, *A Modern Utopia* and *Men like Gods*. Of these the latter stands at the end of the chronological line and is considerably watered by the melodramatic narrative injected into it. The former, and the only one to carry the name in its title, is quite as diluted, this time by exposition, the picture being only a vivid but impressionistic sketch. They also illustrate contrasting methods, as one is distant in time and the other in space.

The god-like men inhabit a planet coincident with ours in space but three centuries ahead of it in time. Two of their young scientists, Arden and Greenlake, decide to make a chemical experiment to see if they can rotate a portion of their universe into the fourth dimension. At this identical moment it chances that Mr. Barnstaple, a London journalist of the early nineteen-twenties, is rambling down the Oxford road with Windsor in the distance, happy in the prospect of a needed vacation. He is unperturbed at being passed by a rude rushing touring car and then by a leisurely polite limousine, but is astounded, as he rounds the corner immediately behind them, to see nothing but a long empty stretch of road. The other cars could have vanished nowhere but into thin air. While gaping over this mysterious disappearance the discomfited driver hears a peculiar snapping sound, has an instant of unconsciousness, and recovers to find himself along with his predecessors in an utterly strange country. For at the precise second that the Arden and Greenlake gates are open, so to speak, these earthlings happen along and are blown in.

They are received into a world of brilliant undefaced beauty and pervasive charm. Everywhere there is clean roomy spaciousness, for although practically the whole globe is under cultivation, its population is kept at about one-fifth of our earth's. The regulated climate permits the people to dress for ornament only, and their reason teaches them to live so sensibly that the man of seventy-three looks like thirty-seven. Their mentality is on a par with Lytton's Vrilya, so that the adolescent school boy is the same mental age as the inferior visitor, Mr. Barnstaple, and is therefore his most congenial companion. They also have ideas for which there are no words in the immigrants' language, and these are communicated largely by radio and telepathy. Yet even such silent messages are not permitted to interrupt the receiver's work. They simply accumulate until collected, and they may be collected by tapping any of the frequent stations.

There might seem in this placid beatific life nothing important enough to suffer from interruption, but it is no less strenuous for being calm and composed. Strongest dynamos run smoothest. For five centuries these people have been energetically civilizing themselves, starting from their Age of Confusion, which corresponded roughly with our present. For this great adventure they rely chiefly on education, the effort to "shape the world anew in the mind of the young." The first lesson is in outwitting Mother Nature and untying her apron strings. "Having taken the old hag in hand, suppressed her nastier fancies, washed and combed her, and taught her to respect and heed this Man, the last child of her wantonings, they were no longer her starved and beaten brats but her free adolescent sons." These sons need no more government among themselves than cooperation by mutual agreement in a sort of guild socialism. Each citizen may have property for use, all he can use, but not a scrap for hoarding or for exploitation. Skilled experts furnish advice in their fields, and the laymen actually take it and act upon it.

Not to be over hopeful, however, Mr. Wells introduces two more or less frictional elements into the situation. The first is the pathetic case of Lychnis, a fine character but a born ministrant and sympathizer whose altruistic impulses have no outlet in a fully capable and self-sufficient society. Endowed with more emotion than mentality, she would be in Jaeger's world a "normal," and in Wells's is a reactionary who cannot feel at home and reconciled to the perfected life.

The second is the atavistic behavior of the accidental guests from the twentieth century, occupants of the cars that out-sped Mr. Barnstaple on the Oxford road. They very soon stop being guests and become blatant promoters. Having brought their own ideas and codes with them, they proceed to organize a revolt whereby they are to get possession of this witless Utopia and convert it into a place which a "real he man" can live and make money in. Their crafty plot is of course frustrated, after some lively incidents, but it serves to indicate the temper of the opposition and to show with what difficulty every inch of progress is won.

In a milder way the Botanist has a similar function in *A Modern Utopia*. His petty egotism is unable to expand itself into larger interests, and his plaintive sentimentality is incapable of a philosophic outlook. This story, the most "central" of Wells's creations, in spite of being scarcely more objectified than Plato's *Republic*, has just the difference from More's *Utopia* that the adjective Modern would signify after a lapse of four centuries. Its modernity consists first and foremost in its size and location. No diminutive island, displaying a snipped-off sample of civilization, could afford scope enough for a twentieth-century scientific imagination. Nothing indeed short of a whole planet would serve.

We are not jolted into this world over an occult crack in the pavement but are wafted in on fancy's miraculous wing. Having entered, we discover that we are on a planet which is the exact duplicate of our earth, except for an improvement that has resulted from a more auspicious trend of history. Beginning with an undefined past, all the latent human capacities have been so fostered instead of obstructed that they are now flowering into full realization. The two mysterious strangers, the Owner of the Voice and his companion the Botanist, are ultimately distinguished from their respective doubles, having been identified by means of thumb-prints and the State's complete card index and registration system accounting for each and every citizen. When the former confronts his, he has the sad satisfaction of seeing himself "as he wished he were, as he might have been, as he could not be," and the more inspiriting pleasure of learning how this better life came about.

In outward appearance it is a replica of other modern Utopias in being a highly mechanized, sleekly operating, healthy and happy life. There is enough official supervision and regulation to promote the welfare of the citizens, but not too much for a free play of individuality. Labor may be a personal enterprise, but the national bureau guarantees employment at a livable wage for a five hour day. Private homes are possible but not popular because club and cooperative living is so much more convenient. Marriage is flexibly monogamous, and motherhood a well paid profession. Business is carried on with a gold currency based on an energy-equivalent. Travel is so easy and so general that the globe's population seems to have reached a new migratory, nomadic cycle. Clothing is also a return to earlier models; the picturesque flowing lines and gay colors of the Italian Renaissance being a favorite with the middle class, a simpler but graceful uniform suiting the workers and students, and the

Samurai alone marked by a designated costume, Hellenic in style.

These Samurai constitute the distinctive feature of this Utopia. They form the ruling class, socially as well as politically. They do not only all the voting and governing but all the judging, doctoring, higher teaching, wholesale employing, and managing of large affairs. This is a frank and thorough aristocracy but it is democratized by the terms of admission. Whosoever will, and can, may become a member of the Samurai. The desire must merely be strong enough to induce the candidate to undergo the probationary discipline and thereafter to live according to the Rule. The discipline is more than monastic in its severity yet its rigorous asceticism is not for the saving of souls but the forging of sterling characters which will in turn become the instruments to forge a firm but supple civilization. Wells elsewhere defies salvation as the completest self-development and self-expression of the individual and thereby of the race. The requirement of a college degree for Samurai is as much for its evidence of persistence and mastery as for the education. This training would naturally qualify them for the occupations mentioned above, but they are by fiat disqualified from certain others, as acting and similar public entertainment, and any form of personal service.

Perhaps the most stringent demand, as it is the most unique, is that each one of the active Samurai must spend one week a year in solitude and under primitive conditions. This going alone into retreat with only the smallest camping kit gives at the same time chance for meditation and proof of sturdy self-reliance and endurance. It is leadership that is expected from this "voluntary nobility" rather than governing, since an intelligent people, with its small percentage of mental unteachables and social incorrigibles segregated on comfortable but detached islands, can capably govern itself. These exiles come from the two lower strata, the "dull" and the "base," while the Samurai are recruited from the two upper, the "kinetic" or intelligentsia, and the "poietic" or creative, gifted with talent or possibly with an erratic transcendent genius.

With all his constructive talent Mr. Wells is not devoid of critical faculty. He has not only committed more Utopianism than any other one man but has also promulgated more Utopian philosophy. This theorizing concerns itself with why and how Utopias should be made, and likewise with why and how they should not. If by his own performances he has set up a target broad as an advertising poster, he has rivalled his own critics in taking shots at it. Not that the critics have been dilatory or faltering. They find this agile gentleman extremely provocative and give themselves the pleasure of saying so with the critic's own candor.

Stuart Sherman, for example, scorns Wells's "hot fit of enthusiasm for social progress excited by fixed contemplation of the Utopian projections of his own fancy," and sneers at his desire "to herd humanity into the Promised Land soon enough to permit him to write a novel called *Beyond Jordan*." Wells might retort that the novel-writing need not wait upon the herding, that in fact it precedes and is supposed to act as an accelerator to it; but he did in effect reply in advance by his spontaneous remark that "the world is not to be made right by acclamation in a day and then left forevermore trusted to run alone." Nothing indeed does he harp upon more than the dynamic nature of the modern ideal in contrast to the static condition of the earlier visions, finished, perfect, and dead.

St. John Ervine in a more dispassionate analysis accounts for the "dreadful depression" of Wells when he confronts this present world, and "the anger which breaks out of his work," on the ground that "The visionary loves mankind in the abstract so much that when he contemplates mankind in the concrete he loses his temper." But Mr. Wells is too sanguine to be depressed, too equable to lose his temper, and too rational in his disposition to see it as an emotional situation at all. There is little in him of a Swift or a Carlyle or a Galsworthy or a Shaw. But there is a good deal in him of the mental architect who loves to draw plans, less for the sake of improving humanity than for the fun of clarifying his own intellect. With a sort of cheerful detachment he appraises this humanity as "inexplicably stupid and lazy and heartless and self-indulgent," and would upon reflection doubtless accept Vernon Lee's amendment that this is all true but the adverb; there is nothing inexplicable about it in the light of man's history.

The whole point of Jaeger's *Question Mark* is its protest against the impossible "inhabitants of the Bellamy-Morris-Wells world." But Wells himself had previously rebuked Morris for supposing we could "make the whole race wise, tolerant, noble, perfect, and wave our hands to a splendid anarchy." Of his own twin planet he says the only alternative would be a Utopia of dolls in the likeness of angels, living under imaginary laws for incredible people; a toy mechanism that would have no appeal for him. He admits that Utopias in general have a tendency to be "hard, thin, and comprehensively jejune," and confesses that he did not name his *Salvaging of Civilization* a Utopia because the word suggests something flimsy and impracticable, agreeable and edifying, no doubt, but of no real value. Yet in another mood he calls his *New Machiavelli* a story of "the white passion of statecraft," and recommends that the state-making vision play a larger part in our fiction, for its stimulating effect. And his own interpretation of the popular antagonisms to Utopia, that it "is a treason to the thing that is,—and usually a slight on the people who are," while a specious half-truth, is apt enough as a rejoinder.

In his latest volume, *Meanwhile,* a character dubbed the Utopographer recites with unquenchable fervor the familiar Wellsian creed that the coming true of the magnificent dream is delayed only by the skeptical apathy of the very ones who could help to make it come true if they only would. Yet this sodden lump is leavened by the few who would if they could. The *Modern Utopia* ends with the bursting of the bubble and a hard bump down to earth. The return to London is as bitter a dose of reality as Bellamy's to Boston. The antidote, however, is not the happy discovery that the return was the hallucination and the other dream the actuality. It is perhaps the more encouraging perception of ideality's germ lurking within the crude but potential fact. On a passing face the traveler glimpsed the Utopian look, and took heart:

"After all, after all, dispersed, hidden, disorganized, undiscovered, unsuspected even by themselves, the *samurai* of Utopia are in this world, the motives that are developed and organized there stir dumbly here and stifle in ten thousand futile hearts. . . ."

Not so futile, perhaps, echoes a voice across the Atlantic, as Don Marquis observes tersely, "Men could not think of the Almost Perfect State if they did not have it in them ultimately to create the Almost Perfect State."

CHAPTER XII

EXPERIMENTS

Of all the skeptical comments on the buoyant faith of Wells and Company the most ironic are the gallant but abortive attempts to refute the skepticism and confirm the faith. To conclude a tour of Utopia-in-the-Skies with an inspection of Utopia-on-Earth is an unfortunate anticlimax instead of a grand finale. And these dreary fizzles of reality are the more depressing because they were launched as pyrotechnic hopes and glowing expectations.

Utopian colonies have been large in number, small in size, and short in duration. These conditions naturally go together. The enthusiasts for a new order are the objectors to the one in existence, and the dissatisfied souls on this planet are always in the majority, though the most of them stop short of definite rebellion, and still fewer of the rebels turn into active apostles for their own notions of betterment. The fact that with all this discount and subtraction the remainder has been responsible for so many of these constructive trials, recurring in the face of previous failures, is eloquent testimony to the hope that springs eternal in the human breast, and to the coeval despair for which this hope is the present solace and perchance the future remedy.

The size and duration are even more closely connected. As in any organism, length of life is proportioned in a general way to the bulk. Yet these social organisms are not even diminutive units. They are only fractions of a society so integral that an isolated colony is about as independent as an amputated finger. Moreover, their already slender chance of survival is diminished by the internal weakness of a group not trained in efficiency or accustomed to prosperity, and the external pressure from a hostile surrounding girdle. The collapse to which they are preordained is only a question of time.

The several histories of these settlements, religious, esthetic, military, industrial, are so easily available that a repetition here would have little point. Three of them, however, deserve special mention by reason of their direct connection with parallel Utopias on paper. It is a cosmopolitan trio, representing Italian, Austrian, and French efforts to supplement theories by practice.

Giovanni Rossi's contribution is well named *Utopie und Experiment* (published in German translation) and combines the two parts into one exhibit. The front and imaginary view displays the flourishing colony at Poggio al Mare, equipped with labor guilds, commuting gentlemen-farmers, free music, drama, library, used and appreciated by all, and bathed in an atmosphere of sunny satisfaction. The rear and actual view exposes the struggling Cittadella, glooming along in Lombardy until it fades out and the promoter goes abroad, awakened by a belated determination to learn something about world politics.

Theodor Hertzka, eminent economist and authority on currency, protested that his *Freiland* was "not the idle creation of an uncontrolled imagination, but the outcome of earnest sober reflection, and of profound scientific investigation." His object was to share his momentous discovery how to transform interest, profit, and rent, into wages and income without descending to communism. His intense delight in this possibility robbed him of the calm needed for abstract presentation.

"Before my mind's eye," he exclaimed, "rose scenes, tangible living pictures of a commonwealth based upon the most perfect freedom and equality, and which needs nothing to convert it into a reality but the will of a number of resolute men. It happened to me as it may have happened to Bacon of Verulam when his studies for the *Novum Organum* were interrupted by his vision of *Nova Atlantis*." For the first part of the story the spokesman is Karl Strahl, who attends the preliminary conference at the Hague, where the eager assent and breathless enthusiasm are voiced in cries of "Forward!" and "Today rather than tomorrow!" Some measure of capital, brains, and culture are prerequisites for membership, and the carefully selected personnel is of superior grade.

From this point the tale is continued by Henry Ney, the young engineer in charge of the advance guard. The expeditionary force is a triumphal progress. "All the arrangements were perfectly carried out. There was no hitch anywhere." The natives greeted them with jubilant astonishment and instantaneous assistance. At a ten day fête in Zanzibar all tribes and all colonizing nations vied with one another in welcome. Arrived at Uganda, they were followed by a lavish torrent of immigrants and funds. Laziness and obstinacy were unheard-of. Every inspired proposition was unanimously carried and immediately put into execution.

The third section of this epic is related through letters written by Prince Carlo Falieri, who arrived after Freeland had had a generation of unstinted and marvellous progress. He is impressed with the ease and joy and dignity of living, and with the profuse wealth, every citizen having an ample capital yielding ten percent. The glorious climax occurs about 1925, when eighty-six countries send delegates to an International Congress at Kenia to debate the feasibility of making a World State based on the Freeland Constitution. After all the objections have been heard and squelched, the ayes have it, being able to substantiate their arguments by the spectacle of a million ecstatic people in possession of over twenty million cultivated acres, fifty first-class steamers, and four busy railroads.

This persuasive volume of Hertzka's not only aroused tremendous interest but incited the challenge whether he really meant business or was just writing Bellamite literature. To prove the former, he bought and edited a journal for propaganda, organized societies, got an international council called, and actually started an expedition off for Uganda. The sixteen pioneers who were chosen from some two hundred applicants managed to reach Lamu, but from there on the scouting party had to overcome nature's obstacles of sandbars and monsoons, and human nature's even more formidable barriers of racial pride and duty of self-preservation. For the British were in sufficient command of that part of Africa to make their consent necessary to any new encroachment. This intruder was not only from a rival nation but looked suspiciously socialistic despite Hertzka's denunciation of socialism as the one worst form of government. Encouragement of so dubious a proposition did not seem the wisest policy. The blockade was not lifted, the goal was not sighted, and the Dark Continent had to muddle along without the dynamo that was to generate enough radiance for the rest of the globe.

Yet a sturdy epilogue came from the undaunted Hertzka four years later in the shape of a postscript, *A Visit to Freeland*, with the subtitle *The New Paradise Regained*. This little book was openly a device to raise funds and spur on a lagging cause, but it is suffused with the same old optimism. The new visitor relates with delighted amazement the wonderful estate of this new Eden. By now the only living opponent in their midst is Professor Tenax, who serves admirably to whet the fresh enlightened argument, and to render the death of his opposition the more impressive because it died so hard.

Étienne Cabet's *Le Voyage en Icarie* was the prelude to a far more resolute and expensive voyage and settlement than the others. The imaginary trip is made by the English Lord Carisdall, a guileless youth who is shown around this model colony in the New World, is rapt by the vision of its exuberant success, and with the additional encouragement of his own romance becomes one of the joyous citizens. Cabet was the first Utopian to enhance his narrative by weaving in a personal story and making it a didactic novel, as well as the first to illustrate the contrast between bright fancy and bleak reality; for the first edition of his book appeared in 1840, and the experiment inaugurated in

1848 continued in about half a dozen localities scattered from Illinois to California until nearly the end of the century.

Never did voyager build a more gracious phantom ship, never did captain try harder to steer his craft into a real harbor than did M. Cabet. The book itself is one of the purest Utopias, conforming to every phrase of the definition. Of its three parts, the first is devoted to a detailed unfolding of the living picture, the second to its historical evolution, the third to an exposition of its principles and philosophy. We are conducted through Icaria's "cities and countrysides, villages and farms, lanes, railroads, canals and rivers, studios, schools, hospitals, museums, theaters, amusements, political assemblies;" we see its management of "food, clothing, housing, furniture, marriage, education, medicine, labor, art;" we confront "the abundance and wealth, the elegance and magnificence, the order and union, the concord and fraternity, the virtue and felicity, which are the infallible result of Communism." And while the author modestly disclaims infallibility for himself, offering his ideas that others may improve upon them, he does maintain that his volume is "the fruit of long toil, immense research, and constant meditation," and therefore deserves not a casual perusal but a patient and thorough study fully to be appreciated.

It had perusal enough, of whatever sort (along

with other circumstances) to rally the disaffected around Cabet's leadership and to launch the emigration to Texas. From New Orleans the pioneers had to make the long overland trip on foot, aided only by ox-teams. On arrival they found the million acres promised by a Land Company shrunken to ten thousand and those obtainable only on condition of building a house on each half-section, these plots themselves broken up into disconnected areas and all in bad shape. When to this disappointment was added malaria and other ills, it became evident that this was, if not the finish, at least a false start. The forced "retreat from Moscow" was made in the teeth of famine, sickness, and all manner of distress. Meanwhile, however, reinforcements from France had reached New Orleans, and the combined parties went up the Mississippi and took possession of an abandoned Mormon camp at Nauvoo, Illinois. This colony attained a moderate success that lasted until the schism in 1856 led to the expulsion and heart-broken death of Cabet himself, the whilom ardent prophet and leader of this alluring but forlorn hope. Émile Thirion chose the better part when he portrayed on paper his refutation of Étienne Cabet through his South American Neustria, and let it go at that; for at least he escaped the fate of the modern Icarus who courted a fall by soaring too high on waxen wings. The date of this final collapse, save for another decade of inert bumping along, was 1887, the very year when Bellamy was writing *Looking Backward*.

Just as the majority of Utopian portraitures were not followed by Utopian practices, so the most of the colonies dispensed with any prefatory scripture of their own, drawing their inspiration from the apocalypse of others. Of these, a South American episode is especially interesting. Over in Australia a man named William Lane was so influenced, and so influenced others, by Blatchford, Bellamy, Hertzka, and their kind, that he managed to establish a settlement in Paraguay, where the Jesuits had once maintained an autocratic communism, and was in fine fettle to "teach the world a lesson." In getting a start he fared far better than Cabet. The colonists were given by the Paraguan government nearly six hundred square miles of fertile land, with lumber and other products. But the fair start promptly petered out into dissension and incompetence. Lane was ousted because he expelled the drunkards. Seceding with a band of followers from New Australia he tried again at Cosme. Finally discouraged by its fiasco he returned to Sydney and his newspaper, after an absence of six years, and the expiring colonies took on a new lease of life under the old individualism.

North America has been the scene of dozens of these ephemeral spurts, involving greater outlay and in the end greater loss. Fourier's Phalansteries

EXPERIMENTS

dotted not only Brazil and Guatemala but New England. Brook Farm, the most picturesque of these, is dryly immortalized by Hawthorne; and Fourier himself was the stimulus to Zola's *Travail*, and later to Ammon's *Das Ei des Kolumbus*, whose scene is in New York.

Our most prominent crusader was Robert Owen. Convinced by his success at New Lanark, Scotland, that the securing of ideal conditions was "the most easy of all practices," he crossed the Atlantic lilting his "sanguine expectations of a speedy and extensive change." He was sure that "with means thus ample to procure wealth with ease and pleasure to all, none will be so unwise as to desire the trouble and care of individual property." After he had sunk thousands of dollars in the hospitably receptive soil of Indiana, the change took place, but it was in his own mind. The difference between his confident desire and the reality was summed up by his son in his account of New Harmony, making a pungent antithesis: "He wanted honesty of purpose and he got dishonesty. He wanted temperance and instead he was continually troubled by the intemperate. He wanted industry and he found idleness. He wanted cleanliness and found dirt. He wanted carefulness and found waste. He wanted to find desire for knowledge but he found apathy. He wanted the principles of the formation of character understood and he found them misunderstood. He wanted these good qualities combined in one and all the individuals of the Community, but he could not find them, neither could he find those who were self-sacrificing enough to prepare and educate their children to possess these qualities."

This elegy might serve also as an epitaph for all these buried hopes which died young, but not because the gods loved them, and which now lie as mute as so many mounds in a cemetery. Monotonous as are their inscriptions, two more bespeak for themselves an extra glance because their requiems were sung by the chief mourners and with quite an unobituary frankness.

Their spasmodic activities took place on the two borders of our continent, Massachusetts and California, about a generation apart. New England in the mid-century was teeming with such enterprises. Emerson wrote to Carlyle: "We are all a little wild here with numberless projects of social reform. Not a reading man but has a draft of a new community in his waistcoat pocket." Mr. Aden Ballou, founder of the Hopedale Community, was warned by Ellery Channing of the very troubles which later did upset his frail canoe of state. Nevertheless he paddled bravely out and navigated his joint-stock company until swamped by the "irretrievable disaster that terminated its existence." This final catastrophe was precipitated by the refusal of the two good business men in the lot to sacrifice further their own interests and carry the helpless bunch on their strong shoulders. The real cause of the disruption, however, Ballou admitted to be the demand of the ultras for the purer communism which would also be more profitable for them. He granted that "the feeble and less productive classes among us were the only gainers." Nor could he reap any consolation from the domestic and intimate side of communal living. "Having entered" (he confessed) "upon the commonplace realities of closely associated life and become familiar with the details and drudgery of daily activities, as well as with each others' personal peculiarities, many of our dreams vanished utterly while others lost not a few of their illusory charms." The disappointed sponsor was candid enough to declare that in spite of the death-like chill that almost froze his heart, his mortification and grief, he "would not lift a finger to save such a Community from its legitimate, predetermined fate."

It was a similar lamentation that arose from Mr. Burnette Haskell in his *How Kaweah Failed*. This colony filed a claim on government timber land in the Sierra Mountains, and had all the needed resources for making a good living. But the living never was made, for "instead of the fraternal, friendly feeling hoped for, one found Kaweah divided into factions and fractions of factions." The result was "absolute anarchy tempered by occasional streaks of despotism." This gave free rein to the loquacity which is a prized inalienable right. Haskell remarked disgustedly that he had seen "a woman getting in firewood with an ax and bucksaw in plain sight of thirteen men gathered for six solid hours around a stump excitedly discussing a rule of order improperly construed at the last meeting." Meanwhile the lumber mill was running at less than ten percent of its capacity, and the honorable operators were loafing "with their mouths full of phrases about living on the spiritual plane and loving your brother." And so this promoter was obliged to conclude that flat failure was the just desert of "those who had believed that they would be the burglars of Paradise," rueful as he was over a ruin that could befall where there had been no evil intent, no malice, no crime nor immorality: nothing, it might be added, but that irresponsibility which is immorality's other name.

These experimental colonies were so many pitiful little Ishmaelites, all under the delusion that they were the original Abrahams chosen to inherit the Promised Land. Even when they were willing to earn their possession they found their Conquest of Canaan too hard a task for such puny uncorrelated methods of attack. That does not mean it might not succumb to more adequate tactics. Isolated communities are now more handicapped than ever, but on the other hand more prevalent and approved than ever before is the spirit of cooperation they tried to capture.

One of our satirists has remarked that Utopians have been embarrassed by want of illustrative material. On the contrary, they have been unembarrassed by its presence. All these futilities spread on the records have no inhibiting power over their imaginative faiths. But even if the reports sent in from the ground-floor of reality have so far contradicted the "News from Nowhere" called by one hearer "real news," they may not always be so contrary. The tune the idealists whistle to keep their courage up is "Work for the Morn is Coming." Some work at reeling off the panoramic cinema of their ideal; others at transmuting the ideal into the real. Their activities may not hasten the dawn, but they can scarcely retard it. In either event the watchers are not to be caught napping.

When the Penny Philosopher in Ashbee's *Thelema* remarked,—"Utopias are always discovered in summer, freeze in snow and are spoiled by rain. They are very easily wetted and then their color comes off:" he was referring to imaginative creations. The statement is even more true of the actual embodiments. But in this fantastic story the symbolism ends on the note of encouragement. The young adventurer in the land of whimsy has to choose between Ralph Hythloday and Lemuel

Gulliver (idealist and satirist). The former won his allegiance, and in return gave him the courage of his convictions. For when he wakes up in London, having had to use the return ticket of his round-trip excursion, his gray disenchantment is brightened by the rainbow of promise: "The vision of Thelema, the reconstructed city of the dreamers of all ages, faded from him, and the scorning voice of the little disagreeable man stung him as it rang in his ears. 'You fool! You damned little fool! I told you there was no such place and that you'd never get there! There never is and there never will be!' But Ralfe knew better."

But Ralfe knew better. He knew there would be such a place and that he would get there. And he undoubtedly would add by way of itinerary, "First through the realm of constructive idealism and and then into the territory of idealistic construction." Or he might quote Emerson's reminder that "practical schemes and workable plans" are always preceded by "totally impracticable dreams and utopian societies."

CHAPTER XIII

SOUVENIRS OF THE TRIP

It is with a queer assortment of ideas and impressions that one returns from an excursion through this intricate universe of human ideals. Many of them are still in the interrogative stage. To find answers of a sort for some of these questions may serve to shake the whole jumble into a fairly intelligible pattern. And to come away without the pattern, after such extensive object-lessons in order and system, might argue a certain denseness in the observer. Merely to avoid the ironic inappropriateness of taking a muddled leave, the traveller should conjure up as coherent and definite a response as possible to the whole Utopian spectacle.

Since Utopia is one form of Applied Hedonism, the foremost inquiry is into the nature of happiness; its constituents and the terms upon which it may be secured. The old abstract—and absurd—question, Is life worth living? is altered to the pragmatic and intelligent, What kind of a life is worth living? And what will it cost?

The Utopian reply is by no means unanimous, but with all the difference of opinion as to means, there is substantial agreement about the end. The end is the better life, and better means more protected and tranquil, more stabilized and harmonious. That this conception is more negative than positive is due to the fact that hitherto all Utopia has been only the first stage of improvement upon reality. Its empyreal heights may have been attained by sudden flight but height is a matter of relativity. Utopia's present level is far from being the last reach in loftiness. When you are repudiating intolerable conditions, the first step is to establish the merely tolerable. This should serve in turn as a useful temporary landing and take-off for altitudes of positive enjoyments and vivid exultant satisfactions.

The present Utopian plane is one of faith in environment and reliance on the more socialized institutions. A powerful but beneficent government guarantees first a well-born citizenry and then to the entire population an adequate education, due measures of labor and leisure, as much beauty and art as it desires, as much morality and religion as it needs, and as much home and family as seem to be good for it. As for the price of these blessings, Utopians are blithe about the low cost of good living, estimating it at the trifling expense of personal liberty, itself a doubtful blessing at best, an injurious bane at its worst, and for the rest largely a myth anyway.

Utopia being a man-made world cannot transcend the human tools and materials of its construction. Its builders were not wizards with esoteric information and magic wisdom; and were therefore subject to the ignorances and limitations of their respective times. They were often prophetic on the mechanical and inventive side, and they sometimes evince a shrewd common sense quite the opposite of chimerical and fantastic, but their anticipations have been of the imaginative order rather than the scientific or intellectual. Their common fallacy has been a credulous idealization of human nature, but they have had to dream without much benefit of psychology, sociology, or anthropology. Since our future Utopians will have a richer mental equipment to start with, much more will be expected of them.

To predict their accomplishments in the way of bigger and better Utopias is another Utopian venture, with the same privilege of being offered for what it may be worth. One safe assertion is that these futurists will be less romantic and more realistic regarding the human stuff out of which all credible Utopias must be constructed. But that does not mean they will be less optimistic as to the ultimate product. By whatever roads they reach their various goals, they will all be routed through the research laboratory, where they will discard surmise and divination in favor of expert testimony and validated theses. And for conjectures as to what Man may become they will substitute conclusions as to what he must become, in view of what he already is, in order to fulfill his best capacities and attain his highest destiny. The double jointed rule that only Utopian people can produce and live in a Utopia, and that only a Utopia can generate and sustain a Utopian people, seems at present to be revolving in a vicious circle. But once reversed into a virtuous revolution, the dextral rotation would be as automatic and permanent as the sinistral.

How to bring about this reversal is the problem. The most hopeful prospect of it comes of course from the evolutionary view. The disclosure that the vast majority of human adults are still children mentally and emotionally is not a verdict of doom but the sign on a milepost. We are not a "race of poor boobs" but of unlicked cubs. After eons of sluggish halting growth we are approaching racial adolescence. Hence we are absorbed in the personal and immediate and preoccupied with the sensuous and sensational. But with one hand clutching our juvenile toys we are with the other grasping at the prizes of maturity. Having stumbled and fumbled our way thus far, and being still alive and husky, we might seem to have fair chances for growing up, especially since we are favored with continually more help and less hampering. This is the time to page the Utopian and deliver to him a request for his list of our best millennial traits together with directions how to increase and develop them.

At the head of this list, as the chief index of maturity, we shall undoubtedly find placed a sense of justice, with a footnote admitting its elusive nature. Utopia itself had its historical origin in an attempt to define justice. Socrates plumed himself on bagging his game, but to those who have been hot on the trail ever since it seems that the quarry is still at large and laughing over its shoulder at its flushed and panting pursuers. The academic definition is, however, less important than a general practice of equity and square dealing. And that is a mark of the transition from youth to manhood. Justice is a rational policy, and the prevalence of injustice comes from our emotional human reinforcement of nature's obvious disregard for rights and privileges. Everybody is fond of shouting "Let justice be done though the heavens fall!" And everybody is wary of doing it for fear they may fall on him. The discovery that it pays better in the long run is one fruit of education.

Education will be the sector of man's environment upon which our new Utopia will lay the greatest stress. And as the School expands, adding more training in ethics and esthetics, the State will shrink on the mandatory side, although it too will increase its constructive operations, on the sound business principle of doing big things on a big scale.

The phase known as "Charities and Corrections" will be obsolete, along with the jingo and the quack. Political Science will be more scientific than political, instead of the other way around, and such direction as is expedient will be through the Expertocracy.

This socializing of what really are common concerns will leave a wide scope for those which are naturally individual. For each man his work, his play, and his home, will offer a maximum of personal liberty and a minimum of restraint and dictation. This will bring more zest into the toil, more active participation into the amusements, and more values of every kind into the home. For the Utopia of the future will provide as much freedom *from* as did its elders, and much more freedom *to*. It can do this without risk of danger because of the improved breed of humanity and its adequate training in the use of independence. There will be none of the old illusion about the plasticity of adult human beings, but there will be a new realization of human nature's infinite potentialities, and a practised technique in converting them into actualities.

This assumption that Utopianizing, so far from being a defunct project, is a live enterprise backed by an enormous capital of confidence, vigor, and wisdom, may be dogmatic; but it is no more so than the opposite declaration that the universe is running down, and no help for it. The poor we may not always have with us. We are beginning to have hopes of expunging poverty and its crew of ills. But it will be worse than a cold day when we no longer have the crusaders with us, and find ourselves bankrupt in idealism.

The Utopian's business is designing advance patterns and selecting attractive goals. He has little interest in the sentiment, "We Don't Know Where We're Going but We're on Our Way," and he sees little use in milling around until you are choked in your own dust. It is a less interesting process than the feeling of progress from point to point. Whether or not there is a far-off divine event, and whether creation may be moving toward it as the train into the station or the bud into the flower, may be mere speculation, but there is no more practical issue than in what direction man is bending his own energies. As an incisive questioner puts it, "Seeing that Man is gifted with foresight and volition, why the deuce should he not apply them to arranging a more tolerable earth? And the more since the worship of the future is the only religion left to us."

As a religion this residue has no superiority to that which the last statement implies to have been discarded, for its object is not even a hallucination. Divinity may not exist, but the future does not. And when that hollow nullity known as the future takes on substance and contour by becoming the present, it may be anything but worshipful. Of course the real meaning of Vernon Lee's conclusion is that an ardent devotion to humanity is religion in the larger vaguer sense, and that it may be expressed by planning in the present a future for the race which can command our pride if not actual adoration. The plans must, to be sure, be put into execution. That is, this is a creed which says its prayers with deeds as well as words.

The actual workers in this fold are those who think in planetary terms, who recognize local and temporary nostrums for social ills as the inane makeshifts they are, and who aim to contribute their mite to the one great cause instead of squandering it on petty and futile side issues. The great cause, on the other hand, may be only a huge nebulosity, on which our petty attacks are quite as futile. There is something in the resigned plaint, "All things have their place in this miserable world, even the pathetic desire of making the world better." But quite aside from any objective achievement, those who are animated by that desire are the least pathetic of human beings. Starting with the formula Eugenics plus Euthenics equals Eutopia, they are committed to inching this world into Eutopia, absorbed in an immense project, drawn on by a quenchless hope. And while there is hope there is life. And so when the Utopia-makers, whether in dreams or deeds, heave ho and go at it, they are getting the best brand of personal satisfaction in the process of furthering a more satisfactory life in general. In conquering the big loutish sulky savage in human nature that resents being civilized, they have the triumph of routing an opponent worthy of their steel.

The routing, in so far as it may be accomplished, will consist in doing away with the lowest of the three classes into which humanity is at present divided. It consists now of the preordained failures, the hovering potentials, and the inevitable successes. When the first have been effaced, and a step-lively passage kept open between the second and third, we may begin to congratulate our Utopians and ourselves. The applause will not be for facile incantations but for downright hard work. And only the few, the very very few, who are endowed with the qualities necessary for initiating and sustaining any advancement, will be in line for receiving the bouquets.

Some doubt has been expressed as to whether there ever will be any bouquets. Sir George Lewis was a spokesman when he said, "No scheme of a perfect or ideal state has worked its way into the general approbation of the civilized world." One cause of this failure to please was explained beforehand by Lord Bacon in an astronomical simile: "Utopias are like stars; they give little light because they are so high." And a similar accounting was afterward added by Robert Lynd when he noted that in the popular view Utopia "is a toy, not a destination."

To many of the Utopians themselves their creations were toys, carved in sportive mood, but for all that they embodied hints and suggestions of what seemed desirable in the way of human destinations. From a cosmic viewpoint any chance of an ultimate destination does indeed look dubious. What the small lad said of the ocean might be applied to the universe: "It is just swimming round and round." And when we consider it from a historical perspective and remember that our own globe, so lightly afloat in its ether, well nigh might swim in the tears and blood shed by its own denizens, we are constrained to wonder if it ever can beget any life worth its heavy price. If it ever can and does, the improvement, already germinant indeed, will be speeded up by a wider broadcasting and a deeper permeating of such diagnoses as have been made of the common human malady.

"We shall never even begin our journey toward the Delectable Mountains of the Perfect Society or the Ideal Republic," observed A. E. Wiggam, "until man is regarded honestly, straightforwardly, and upon the basis of experimental knowledge, as the strange, interesting, contradictory, childish and noble, but ultimately measurable, weighable, and predictable being that he is."

SOUVENIRS OF THE TRIP

"An outline of human aspiration is a logical and harmonious addition to our literature," says Archibald MacLeish in commenting on Lewis Mumford's *Story of Utopias;* and adds, "One of our greatest needs is to know what we want. Individually we want fervently, extensively, insatiably. But socially we want, if we want at all, half-heartedly, aimlessly, and without agreement of purpose." The Utopians may lack agreement among themselves, but they are neither half-hearted nor aimless. And they would continue the analysis by noting that a sense of need is futile without a sense of direction. And that implies the challenge,—If you don't like the other fellow's goal, where is your own?

The searchlight illumination comes from the cosmically external view. So long as we Earthians are one big though unamalgamated family we have no human-racial ambition, nothing beyond personal or national pride. The only thing that could really put us on our mettle would be the judgment of an entirely outside tribunal, based on an interplanetary competition. By such a standard would we be haughty or humiliated? It is to be feared that the Empyreal Visitor so frequently invoked by the Utopian wand would be most amazed by the discrepancy between opportunity and achievement in this our world. He would behold a tribe called Mankind marked by a congenital craving for happiness and an enormous capacity for it. This race is born into an auspicious environment, on a beautiful and bountiful earth whose natural offerings are marvellously and increasingly supplemented by the discoveries and inventions of its population. Where, then, is the happiness? Why is this so potential planet not by this time a kinetic accomplishment, a land of fulfilled desire, a materialized Utopia?

The answer is that its inhabitants are marked also and equally by heavy inertia, lack of sympathetic and vicarious imagination, and a clinging fondness for the status quo. Most fatal of all is the fact that any objection to that status comes from those who are uncomfortable in it. So long as the under dog can only whine or growl his futile protest unheeded by the secure and indifferent upper dog, so long will the established order prevail. It takes both heart and brain, vitalized by will, to institute a change for the better. As a rule, the under dog is short on brain, and the upper on heart. The saviors of society must be endowed with all good things, and the rarity of that combination makes them the saving remnant.

"Our first parents were shoved out of Eden backward," remarks Patrick Quinn Tangent in *The New Columbia*, "and their descendants haven't had gumption enough to turn around." However, since necessity is the mother of gumption, the one may force the other on us in the course of time.

"In our own age even Utopias affect the spirit of

legislation," opines Benjamin Jowett, confirming Lamartine's "Utopias are often only premature truths," and reinforced by Oscar Wilde's "Progress is the realization of Utopias."

Even the skeptical Anatole France concedes that "Without the Utopias of other times, men would still live in caves, miserable and naked." And his conclusion,—"Out of generous dreams come beneficial realities. Utopia is the principle of all progress, and the essay into a better future,"—receives an appropriate amendment in Vida Scudder's tart observation: "Time was when our flight into the future might have been judged of the Icarus variety, borne by wings sure to melt as they soared. But we are less scornful of flying than we were." Robert Lynd also reckons on inevitable evolution in his argument:

"There is as much reason for a Negro to shrink from the life of an English peer as for an English peer to shrink from the life of a Utopian. The peer, however, has slowly adapted himself to the austere earthly paradise in which he dwells. He can even look back without longing to that occasional breakfast of human rashers which his ancestor of ten thousand years ago would not have given up for a world of Utopias. He misses all these little failings of his fathers, indeed, as little as the Utopian of ten thousand years hence will miss the little failings which most of us nowadays treasure as the sacred elements of our personality. The English peer and the England of today are, however, but the Utopian and the Utopia of the stunted aborigine of ten thousand years ago. Seeing that the peer is not afraid to live in his giddy perch high above the aborigine, why should modern man dread the thought of existence in a still giddier perch somewhere above the peer?"

Without pausing for a reply to his pungent rhetorical question, Mr. Lynd proceeds to a diagnosis which succinctly packs militant Humanism and applied Utopianism into the same nutshell and hints how they might expand into a cooperative accomplishment. "I have a terrible conviction," he exclaims, "that if the human race in peace had ever been willing to undergo half the sacrifices which it was willing to undergo in time of war, we should have had Utopia painted on the map of the world long ago."

CHAPTER XIV

POSTSCRIPT

This aftermath is in the nature of an informal appendix, containing brief annotations and data that did not fit in under the headings of the preceding discussion. One item that might be welcome to those interested in the subject is some information about certain of the Utopians.

As authors they fall into three classes: the obscure, the somewhat distinguished, and the eminent. One disparaging critic has defined Utopias as "literary curiosities made respectable by illustrious names." These names—presumably Plato, Xenophon, Plutarch, More, Bacon, Fénelon, Cooper, Hale, Lytton, Hudson, Morris, Zola, Anatole France, Wells, Howells—have been sufficiently blazoned on biographical records. Since their Lives have been so capably written and made so accessible that a repetition would be superfluous, they may be brought upon this particular stage with the familiar formula that they "need no introduction." The negligible names, at the other extreme, also need none, but for the opposite reason. In the literary middle class, however, stand a few of the Utopian contributors who deserve to have their limited renown expanded by at least a special mention in this connection. Among these are Andreae, Campanella, Harrington, Mercier, Restif, Spence, Blatchford, Benson, Tardé, Sweven, Merejkowski, and House.

Johann Valentine Andreae was a German of wealth, culture, and energy. Preacher, teacher, and writer, he established at Calw a cooperative community of his own students and parishioners. Later he enlisted the workmen and founded an industrial organization that had a long and successful career: The Weavers' and Dyers' Mutual Protective Association. Meanwhile he wrote *One Hundred Satirical Dialogues* and *Images of the Virtues and Vices of Human Life,* besides the poem which was the earlier version of his *Christianopolis.* This four-square city of only four hundred inhabitants, on the triangular island Caphar Salama only thirty miles around (in contrast to Bacon's Bensalem five thousand miles in circumference), was constructed not as a magical plan but as able to "lessen the burden of our mortality." And its architect, though often dryly humorous, was in earnest when he exclaimed, "Oh may I sometime see better, truer, more fixed and more stable conditions—in brief, those which the world promises but never and nowhere produces!"

Thomas Campanella, although an orthodox Dominican monk and befriended by Pope Urban VIII and Cardinal Richelieu, was caught in a Spanish trap and spent twenty-six years in a dungeon at Naples. His *City of the Sun* was, like *Pilgrim's Progress*, a product of prison life. He also wrote a number of poems and metaphysical treatises.

James Harrington was likewise arrested and imprisoned on an unfounded charge of treason, and though his confinement was short it was enough to unbalance his mind for the rest of his life. He had been a member of the royal court and fulfilled the sad office of attending Charles I to the scaffold. Thereafter he was interested in reconstruction and put into his *Oceana* his ideas of a practicable republic. Four years later, along with the Restoration, came Henry Stubbe's burlesque, *The Commonwealth of Oceana*, which ridiculed Harrington, even as he himself had taken issue with Hobbes's *Leviathan*. It is interesting to note that as early as the middle of the seventeenth century he was prophesying a strong and rebellious America.

Louis Sébastien Mercier was a Girondist at the French National Convention, and was called "too advanced for Robespierre." He became Professor of Rhetoric at the College of Bordeaux, and wrote a number of plays, romances, and essays, including the satiric *Pictures of Paris*. His own picture of Paris in 2440 (advanced in the English translation to 2500) is serious and naive. But along with its sentimental rhetoric it has sound sense and shrewd suggestions. One engaging idea might repay modern consideration. Every man writes a book of his life and thoughts, which is read aloud at his funeral as his obituary. Obsequies are celebrated as happy occasions in true Utopian style.

Nicolas Anne Edmé Restif de la Bretonne was a friend of Mercier's and was said in his ideas to reach back to Rousseau and forward to Balzac and Zola. In his career he advanced from peasant to printer and prolific romancer. He called his *Southern Discovery by a Flying Man or The French Daedalus* "a very philosophical novel." It is a riotously fantastic tale in three parts, the Utopian being saved till the third, in which Megapatagonia is discovered. Nearly a decade after the *Homme Volant* came the author's *L'an Deux-Mille*. Written during the early part of the Revolution, this play shows how Louis XVI averted that catastrophe by summoning a second States-General and turning the tide toward peace, and how two centuries later Louis François XXII is presiding over a gladsome, sentimental, military communism.

Thomas Spence, book-seller in High Holborn, designer of symbolic coins, writer of radical pamphlets, was twice consigned to Newgate for his ill-timed activities. He is credited with being the originator of Paine's famous phrase, The Rights of Man, and he illustrated those rights in his semimetaphoric *Spensonia*. This is "a country in fairyland, situated between Utopia and Oceana." The story ends with a sharply ironic recantation.

Robert Blatchford, author of *Merrie England* and editor of *The Clarion*, was, although so near the end of the list, the first to build his Utopia (and a bright and gay one it is) out of a personal experience of deprivation and hardship. His notions of a remedy may be fanciful but his knowledge of a remedy-needing situation was not academic. One who has spent his childhood running errands twelve hours a day for thirty-five cents a week, and who has been cold, hungry, and tired most of the time for years, will be well grounded in his sympathies at least. Nor is he ill grounded in his logic when he asserts that "It is only reasonable to suppose that in a wisely ordered commonwealth the best energies of a trained and intelligent people would be directed toward the improvement of all the conditions of national, civic, and domestic life." His *Sorcery Shop* is well subtitled "An Impossible Romance" and its sentimental extravagance is easy to parody in a *Newaera*, but there is something contagious in his enthusiasm when he exults that his people are "Happy, happy, happy!"

Robert Hugh Benson was the third distinguished son of a distinguished father, the Archbishop of Canterbury. Like his older brothers, Arthur Christopher and Edward Frederick, he was educated at

Cambridge, but unlike them, he became a Catholic (when past thirty years of age) and later entered the priesthood. No Dryden nor Newman could outdo him in the zeal of a proselyte, and his trenchant contrast between a future disastrous under Protestantism and magnificent under Catholicism is a unique and effective testimony to the power a man's convictions may have over him.

Gabriel Tardé was Professor of Modern Philosophy at the Collége de France, a noted criminologist, and author of many volumes and many more articles on various aspects of sociology, economics, and philosophy. In his *Underground Man* he plays and invites his fancy, to the great delectation of himself and his audience. Looking backward from the sixth century of the Era of Salvation, he recalls how in the twenty-fifth century A. D. the sun had grown cold and the earth was a dark frozen orb swinging lifelessly through space. Lifeless, however, only on the surface, for the saved remnant of humanity, shivering in their last resort at Babylon, the world capital, hit upon the plan of digging in, and excavating a new habitation under the sheltering crust of the old. Here, snugly ensconced, protected by a roof that never leaks, warmed and lighted by free electricity, fed by chemical products and by their mammoth cold storages, these Neo-Troglodytes have instituted a Geniocratic Republic wherein progress is stimulated by sympathy and admiration instead of envy and rivalry. They had started with a superior stock, for before they were driven from earth's surface they had established a World State and compelled their fit to survive by forbidding them all military service. So now freed from commercialism, journalism, and such nuisances, they are devoting themselves to the development of their highest emotional, intellectual, esthetic, and imaginative faculties. Any incipient hankering for the old life is readily squelched by turning on a phonograph record of the sounds rife at that time.

Colonel Edward House wrote his *Philip Dru* as the pastime of a gentleman with a taste for politics, and published it anonymously. It is an interesting coincidence that this friend of Woodrow Wilson issued in 1912 a book whose story starts in 1920. Colonel House visualized a young West Point graduate, aglow with social sympathy and a sense of justice, heading a revolution at that date. An easy conquest of the reactionary forces was followed by a mild dictatorship to tide the country over the crisis. In 1935 Dictator Dru, satisfied with the working of his conservatively liberal regime, withdrew voluntarily and took himself off to Europe. In connection with this tale a later French story should be mentioned. This is Follin's *La Révolution des Quatre Septembre*, a slight allegoric postwar reconstructive picture featuring Woodrow

Wilson, the only character who operates under his own name.

When a year ago the Oxford University Press published new editions of *Limanora* and *Riallero,* the mysterious Godfrey Sweven was revealed as John Macmillan Brown, born in Scotland, Professor Emeritus of Classic and English Literature at Canterbury University College, Chancellor of the University of New Zealand since 1923, and author of several volumes of literary criticism besides a series of accounts of the South Seas.

Dmitri Sergeievich Merezhkovsky is a versatile Russian whose complete works fill many volumes and embrace many forms of literature. He is poet, essayist, critic, translator, dramatist, and novelist. It is by his fiction that he is best known, especially the trilogy of romances entitled *Christ and Antichrist.* Each of these three volumes centers around an historical figure: *The Death of the Gods* dealing with Julian the Apostate (as does Ibsen's *Emperor and Galilean* in his series on a similar theme), *The Forerunner* with Leonardo da Vinci, and *Peter and Alexis* with Peter the Great. About the same time he was doing his bit for idealism in a volume which was translated into German by H. Mordaunt under the caption, "*Das Irdische Paradies,* Ein Märchen aus dem 27 Jahrhundert. Eine Utopie von C. von Mereichkowsky."

This Earthly Paradise is located on an island near

POSTSCRIPT 289

Tahiti, and the involuntary visitor reaches it by drowning. From his oblivion he awakens to a sunrise scene in a pastoral glade, where the population is up and frolicking before breakfast. The stranger is taken in hand by the aged Jesrar, who identifies him by his costume, a replica of the outlandish exhibits in the nineteenth century room of the museum of antiquities. For a day this human relic dwells in the pristine yet philosophic Eden of the future, but the next morning he is aroused from a ghastly nightmare to find himself back in the cold dreary world of reality. His revolt against its drudgery, poverty, war, and terror is voiced in the final anguished cry of mankind: "Will you never let this wonderful dream come true?"

In such instances as the above it is the Utopia-maker that is awarded the special mention. There are other instances where the creation is of more importance than its creator. These also belong to the middle group lying between the prominent and familiar and the trivial and negligible. Several and sundry of these Utopias either boast of their little points of distinction or are difficult of access by reason of being untranslated from their foreign language or because of the rarity of copies. Such of these as seem worth more than a mere unidentifying enumeration are hereby given their bare rescue from oblivion.

The majority of these, as it happens, form a

small Utopian subdivision by themselves, and a peculiar one at that. Its unifying bond is in the method used by the writers, the plan of literally looking backward upon a reconstructed state of affairs, or things as they might have been. The sketching in of a pseudo-historical background is indeed a general Utopian practice and a first aid to plausibility, even if the story is located in the present or the future. But this idealized history and romanticized biography is a more definite device. It began in the beginning, with the Greeks, for that is the framework of Plato's *Critias*, Plutarch's *Lycurgus*, and Xenophon's *Cyropaedia*, this last being in part a reply to *The Republic*, and in turn the source of a long thin trickle of Cyrusian legend.

Its modern representatives start in the seventeenth century with Anton le Grand's *Skydromedia*, Harrington's *Oceana*, and Fénelon's *Télémaque*. This last, composed as an inspirational tract for the court tutor's royal pupil with a view to making the dauphin's coming reign Utopian, becomes ironic in the light of the Duke of Burgundy's untimely death and the subsequent fate of the French throne. The twenty-four books of Fénelon's "Matter of Troy" constitute his sequel to the *Odyssey*, but the Utopian episode is confined to the twelfth and the twenty-second books. It is presented as Mentor's advice to King Idomeneus at Salentum in Hesperia, and is a skillful compound of Plato and

Plutarch with an infusion of the new French socialism.

In the eighteenth century Terrasson's *Sethos* and a trilogy by Haller,—*Fabius and Cato, Usong,* and *Alfred,*—magnify the statesman into Utopian stature. Berington's *Gaudentio di Lucca* is retrospective, (with a covert bit of satire against the Inquisition); and in Brugh's *Cessares* the letters of Herr Vander Neck from the Dutch outpost in western Patagonia to his friend in Holland are dated a century and a half before the book that preserves them.

The nineteenth century list is headed by Ellis's *New Britain*. This English colony is located on the prairies west of the Missouri River, where a settlement was made early in the sixteenth century by a band of two thousand pioneers. It remains a rural community with no cities but one continuous village broadening into occasional towns, and is the rustic prelude to the Morris-Howells idylls.

Its immediate successor, Fox's *New Holland,* expands the same formula. For the identical three century period an isolated settlement has been developing itself in unhampered freedom. At the end of this time it is discovered (as was New Britain by the two Englishmen who followed up the American sea-captain's report) by five explorers who persisted through barren coasts, swamps, lakes, rivers, mountains, deserts, to the broad plateau on a South

Sea island. They find the colony increased from four hundred to four million, with a proportionate advance in civilization.

Thirion's *Neustria,* written to oppose Cabet's *Icarie,* though with no subsequent object-lesson, follows the fortunes of the ex-Girondists who emigrated after the Revolution to eastern Patagonia (adjacent to the earlier Cessares) and named their Capital Charlottesville in honor of Mdlle. Corday. It is a "Utopie Individualiste" yet neither "a Land of Cocagne nor an Ideal Republic, nor sentimental, like Jean-Jacques." By 1840 these pioneers are so prosperous that communistic doctrines fall flat on a contented people. By 1850 they have a population of two million functioning happily under a sound conservation constitution. Mild drama is furnished by the Thomas family, driven from Europe in disastrous 1848, landing on these foreign shores with mixed emotions of hope and fear, taken in charge by a Land Company, conveyed to a farm on the outskirts, provided with house, furniture, implements, stock, garden, and food, all funded as a loan at eight percent. They are given a year of trial before signing up as installment-paying owners; and being a thrifty industrious set, are successful and dumbly grateful for their life of security and self-respect.

The same year produced another French Utopia, Zola's *Travail,* but it opposes Thirion and reinforces Cabet. In this melodramatic romance of communism all capitalists are dastardly villains or wretched weaklings who set fire to their own houses or hang themselves in the garden or are crushed under a suddenly crumbled church or somehow come to the bad end which they have coming to them. The final triumph of the proletariat is voiced in a sweetly warbled melody which cannot be called a harmony because the potential discords have been entirely hushed. Its last grating note is the mutinous Ragu, who turns his back on the vast communal feast and out from Eden takes his solitary way. As a hideous rascal Ragu is an insignificant trifle but as a symbol he is portentous. Like the Botanist in Wells's *Modern Utopia* and Morgana and Christopher in Haldane's *Man's World*, he is the recalcitrant who, whether right or wrong, makes the Utopian problem insoluble.

Thirion's *Neustria* had another kind of parallel in Pemberton's *Happy Colony*, for that too was a second volume written to dramatize and advertise the author's first, which was expository. The practical design was to induce British workmen to take up two hundred thousand acres in New Zealand and organize ten colonies along ideal lines. In spite of his naive fondness for elegance, amiability, and propriety, Pemberton had common sense and advanced ideas.

Common sense and reactionary ideas mark

Cooper's *Crater,* whose story is dated about half a century before the book itself. Only the last third of this romantic novel is Utopian, and even that of a dubious cast. For this South Sea idyl ends with the suddenly upheaved Vulcan's Peak as suddenly submerged, so that the whole experiment was washed away, but not before it had been spoiled anyway by intrusive malign influences.

Like this and several others, Jules Verne's ideal is a small Utopian structure set at the end of a long rambling avenue of approach. Chapter Ten of *The Five Hundred Million of the Begum* tells of the founding in Oregon about 1873 (six years before the book was published) of two rival cities. These are the respective enterprises of the German Herr Schultze and the French Dr. Sarassin, each of whom has inherited a fortune and has this notion of the most exciting way to spend it. It is the super-sanitary, fastidious, exclusive France-Ville that is the Utopia. It is, however, doomed to destruction by its ruthless and tyrannic neighbor, and saved only by the courage and enterprise of the hero, Marcel Bruckmann. After his victory the enemies are reconciled (as in Rosewater's '96) and united into a compromise industrial city called Sthalstadt.

In 1883 a slight sketch by Ralph Centennius (pseudonym for Peterborough) presents *The Dominion in 1983* as if viewing in retrospect the century's achievements. Canada's first achievement was to avert the danger of being merged with the United States. The next was the abolition of taxes in 1945, the country thenceforth being supported by the interest on its capital. Of course there was no more war, poverty, nor disease, and but little crime. Parliament is reduced to fifteen members, one from each province, yet this body represents nearly one hundred million people. Climate is regulated by internal heat and rain is made to order. There is much air travel on "rocket cars," made of calcium bronze and propelled by the gradual expansion of solidified oxygen and hydrogen. This gas is put up in blocks of one hundred horse-power and sold at all drug stores just as so many pounds of sugar at the grocery. A car holds fifty passengers and travels sixty miles a minute. But for ground transportation they still use electric tricycles.

The same year evoked a very different vision in Hellenbach's *Die Insel Mellonta*. In this tale the sole survivor of a shipwreck finds himself in a charming community whose residents wear seventeenth century costumes and speak French. He learns that in 1793 the Marquis of Chateau-Morand, retired officer of the royal marines, with fifty companions and half a million francs, started for Rio Janeiro but landed near Tahiti. The colony thus established carried out the principles of Rousseau and Voltaire, and their descendants were now welcoming their first visitor from the outside world. They adopt him into their village, a continuous garden-plot with cottages set in a triple circle, and appoint him lecturer in nineteenth century history. The lively story carries much philosophic and satiric conversation and considerable romantic adventure. Then at the height of happiness the whole island is destroyed by earthquake and volcanic eruption. This catastrophe is not, however, the end of the story but only of the hypnotic trance into which Alexander has been thrown. He awakens at Delhi and is let into the mystery by the Brahmin Shakretto. The eruption had been produced by a red light and the drowning by a wet towel. More conjuring reveals his Mellonta companions as incarnations of the pictures of Aspasia and Alcibiades and the busts of Plato and Fourier which adorned his room at home. After much grief over the hopeless state of the world Alexander journeys up the Himalayas to try the effect of a cosmic view. This volume antedated *Looking Backward* but the third edition (1896) followed it and contains a note referring to it as a sort of corollary to Bellamy's work.

It was upon the Himalayas that another seeker, Alexander Musgrove, did derive inspiration, because he found there a real Utopia in prime condition. He was the hero of Craig's *Ionia*, a young humanitarian who had undertaken to redeem one of London's worst slums with the aid of a fortune left him by his philanthropic mother. He organizes his social settlement and does his best, but with little effect. When half his money and two-thirds of his faith and courage have been drained away, he is invited by a sympathetic visitor, Jason Delphion, to take a trip with him. An aeroplane carries them to an otherwise inaccessible mountain fastness and deposits them in Jason's native land among some distant cousins of Hale's Sybarites. For it seems that during a campaign of Alexander the Great a band of seven thousand Ionians had been cut off in Persia and had taken refuge on this plateau, reaching it by its single pass, which had since been closed. After a heartening sojourn with this elevated populace the Englishman is able to return and tackle his own problem with renewed strength and increased intelligence.

The Ionians' Hellenic kin, the Sybarites, had been ensconced in the heel of Italy's boot back in the time of Romulus, and there in peaceful isolation the successive generations had embodied the ideal of a true Sybaritism. For this, correctly interpreted, means a demand for a serene and noble existence. By accident this Elysium is stumbled upon by the Reverend Frederic Ingham, en route to Gallipoli on a political errand for Garibaldi. He finds these neo-classic citizens charmingly modern and pioneers in handy inventions. They particularly pride themselves on their little private steam cars heated by petroleum. Every morning these are filled and lighted first thing and thus ready for use right after breakfast.

In *The English Revolution* Lazarus romances about the immediate past, and in *Aristopia* Holford about a period more remote. The latter is labelled indeed "A Romance History of the New World" and centers about the Jamestown of 1607. Near that time and place Ralph Morton has the luck to discover a gold mine, and the wit to keep his discovery to himself, later using his wealth to purchase from James I a charter and a free hand with his colony. This he names "The Best Place" and proceeds to make it fit the name. It develops such resources, natural and human, that in 1776 this superior little state becomes the very backbone of the American Revolution.

Paul Adam's *Lettres de Malaisie* is apparently a by-product of the Spanish-American War. A Spanish diplomat sent to the Philippines in 1895 to quell threatened trouble writes nine long epistles to a friend in France. An apologetic preface by this French recipient and publisher of the correspondence explains that the writer is a brave but artless soul, and opines dryly that the conditions he reveals are far from ideal. In his own introduction Paul Adam himself admits that the picture here presented indicates the logical course of events rather than the most desirable. His personal hope would be for greater individualism, yet he is driven toward socialism in revolt against English and German imperialism. Appearing originally in 1898, the volume was reissued under the title *La Cité Prochaine,* and revived in 1922 with a return to the first title. In this last the author observes that so far the Yankees have accomplished nothing in the Philippines in spite of their lavish expenditures and magnificent gestures.

What the letters depict is an autocratic communism in Borneo, inspired by Cabet's *Icarie* but doing better in the Orient than he did in the Occident. Branches had spread into Mindoro, Mindanao, Iebu, and Negros, on which could be discerned the high landing-towers of the planes by which alone intercommunication was possible. It was, says the Spaniard, these French brothers of his friend who were inciting the Malays to revolt against the rule of Castile. The investigating expedition, of which he was placed in charge, managed by force and fraud to enter the Bornean harbor Amphitrite. It is, however, hospitably received, the time being just ripe for the experimenters to give over their self-protective seclusion and share their success with the world. Since 1843 these disciples of Fourier, Proudhon, Saint Simon, and Cabet have been timorously secretive but now their safety is assured.

The invader is made an official guest of the Dictatorship, supplied with the costume in vogue and started off on a sight-seeing excursion. He finds every modern convenience, including news and entertainment broadcast by the public telephone, (the form taken by Bellamy's prediction of the radio). He is told the story of Jerome the Founder and his first buildings in the order of their importance: Maternity Home, Nursery, School, College, Lyceum, University, Presbytery, and Hospital. The chief cities are Minerve, Jupiter, Mars, Mercury, and Vulcain, each having its own specialty. Jupiter, the City of Power, is ruled by an Oligarchy of Creators. Any inventor, writer, artist, may become a candidate for one of its fifty seats, and hold it for a rather precarious tenure of office. There are also one hundred each of senators and deputies, divided among the professions.

The general impression is of a people at once frankly sensual, exotic, voluptuous, and highly intellectual. Their chariot of pleasure is borne by the two steeds physical revelry and mental reverie, not pulling apart but stepping in rhythmic accord. Passing from emotional orgy to abstruse research, one finds them equally refreshing. By this philosophy the only virtues are production of life and the discovery and invention that make life enjoyable. Conversely, the two sins are destruction of life and refusal to work. Slight drama is injected into the story by the vivacious ladies, Thea and Pythie, who act as the stranger's guides, instructors, seducers, and whatever is necessary to initiate him into their delightful mode of life.

Another French revision of the recent past is *How We Brought about the Revolution,* by Messers. Petaud and Pouget. It is also another "Histoire des Quatre Ans," but as diametric from Halévy's gloomy cataclysm of 1997 to 2001 as that in turn from Bellamy's bright portrait of that very period. The account of these Four Years (ironically enough just preceding the Great War) has the Utopian tone of confident optimism. In every crisis "the people had an intuition of what it was necessary to do." During the transition stage "not a single discordant note came to trouble the atmosphere of good comradeship." An invading European army was sent home without a battle and all was serene on the Seine. Yet after the first effervescence they simmered down to common sense. "The insurgents were not intoxicated with their victory," and in the new regime they were content to work hard for only a moderate reward.

The farthest retrospect is in Hatfield's *Geyserland,* a prolix communistic version of another Polar Sea Utopia which started in the tenth century B.C. And finally, there are three of these historical reconstructions that belong to the essay or disquisition class. Condorcet's *Esquisse d'un Tableau Historique des Progrès de l'Ésprit Humain* is merely an outline to demonstrate the possibility of improvement. Renouvier's *Uchronie* is an elaboration of the same idea: his apocryphal account of European civilization is suggested in the sub-title, "L'Utopie dans l'Histoire;" and starts with the impetus given by Chinese philosophy in the eighth century, makes the influence of Marcus Aurelius the real point of departure, and presents it all through documents collected by three generations of a seventeenth century family. *Phoebus,* by Raoul Heinrich Francé, is further labelled "Ein Rückblick auf das Glückliche Deutschland im Jahre 1980," and follows the usual formula.

The same future date is chosen by Masson for his somewhat symbolic *Utopie des Îles Bienheureuses dans le Pacifique en l'An 1980*. This is one of several idealistic refuges as a post-war reaction, and begins with the migration in 1920 of a group of disillusioned veterans. They colonize three islands to which they assign the young, the mature, and the aged, respectively, but with a free and constant passage back and forth. When after three score years the visitor is ferried over by Chrisnore he meets a race of gentle but vigorous people who have achieved an artistic and altruistic anarchy. They are zealous in good works and adept in the use of inventions. Their food is cooked, if at all, by caloriphore, and their rooms are hinged on pivots in order to follow the sun. The stranger is adopted into the family of Esthio and Esthia, whose sister Giroflee turns out to be the dreamer's own wife, having with their two children preceded him to the isles of the blest.

Among Utopian curiosities should be mentioned *La Ville des Expiations,* published in 1832 by Pierre-Simon Ballanche, and reedited in 1926 by Amand Rostand. Books IV to VII describe a penitential Utopia, wherein the best conditions are provided for culprits and criminals. A modern instance of this plan is developed in Stephen McKenna's *Beyond Hell.*

The special tribute due to Ismar Thiusen's *The Diothas* comes from its date, for it is a Bellamite story that preceded *Looking Backward* by five years. The narrator awakes in the Nuiorc of the ninety-sixth century, is clothed in the current Hellenic style, improved physically enough to pass muster, adopted and shown about by the hospitable Utis Estai, who bears a strange resemblance to his old friend, physician, and hypnotist, back in the nineteenth century. It now develops that young Ismar is from New Zealand and is paying a visit to his distant American relatives, partly to recuperate from a nervous breakdown. This has been induced by a habit of mesmerizing himself and returning in trances to the nineteenth century as a short cut to his historical researches. This prolonged living in a reconstructed past has set up the hallucination that it is the only reality. He is kindly taken in hand and instructed as a patient suffering from lapse of memory. The historical résumé given him is the model for subsequent Utopians: the final war and collapse of civilization in the twentieth century, an interval of barbarism, then slow but sure reconstruction. The present Nuiorc is built on the ruins of the old city now buried and forgotten. Yet its galleried arcades, its continuous sidewalks along the upper levels, its frequent bridges, outdoor stairs and elevators, present a picture not unlike one that appeared in a recent New York Sunday Times as an architect's vision of the probable future. Its electric motors, dictaphones, tachygraphs, telephone-radios, dumb-waiters that send up the food previously ordered from central kitchens and click into the center of the dining table, were novelties at the time of writing. Ismar starts another fashion by falling in love with Riva, who haunts him as the reincarnation of the girl he left behind him. On their wedding trip their motor boat is disabled and drawn over the brink of Niagara Falls. When the hero recovers consciousness he is his old self again with his devoted Edith waiting for him to come out of the trance.

Among the post-Bellamite variants on this theme is Salisbury's *Birth of Freedom*. It relates the desperate situation, the consequent revolution, the wise reconstruction. Forty years later, Cecil Lord, who had been deported as a sympathizer with the wrong side, returns from Exiles' Rest in the Alaskan mines to find New York in high socialistic triumph. The new policy had been compulsory at first, until the people were educated to the point of choosing it voluntarily. It is now 1930, a year that sees transportation being made by air cables, the cars sliding along like enlarged cash boxes in a department store; all factories topped by spacious roof-gardens for the enjoyment of employees; and no taxation except for local improvements. The tale concludes with a belated romance and a splendid symbolic historical pageant representing the Birth of Freedom.

It takes until 1950 for Chavannes' Future Commonwealth to materialize under American sponsoring in Socioland, Africa. The impressed visitor is Samuel Balcom, who writes exuberant letters to his friend Harry about the million people who thrive with a public surplus instead of debt, in spite of free bread, water, gas, hospitals, asylums, and liberal pensions. Land is leased from the State, at no rent but in limited amount.

Among the extra-terrestrial Utopias is Simpson's *The Man from Mars*. In this the visiting formula is reversed and news brought from the far country by a cosmos-trotting inhabitant. He appears to a recluse astronomer on a mountain top, and informs him that Earth is ten thousand years behind Mars in development, so that the Martians have been studying us as interesting primitives. Their advanced race is united and affectionate under a paternal government that provides all the conveniences and pays for them by the single tax on land. There are grades in financial and social sets but no extremes. Workers are judged according to strength, skill, and activity; professional men by talent, intelligence, and capability. The Bureau of Statistics anticipates that of the still remoter Wellsian planet. There are gorgeous public buildings of malleable metal decorated with manufactured gold and diamonds. Roofs of domed glass cover spacious social halls equipped for concerts and dances. All travel is by air, and an equal smoothness marks their communal progress. In this society "it is enough to determine that a measure is for the common good to secure its adoption without dissent."

The more stereotyped method is John Jacob Astor's in his *Journey to Other Worlds*. In that overworked year 2000 he slips across to Jupiter and Saturn, the abode of deceased Earthians. The story is mainly occupied, however, with conditions here on earth. On our gusty planet the climate has at last been equalized by the Terrestrial Axis Straightening Company. The entire western hemisphere is Americanized. New York's population has mounted to fourteen and a half millions. Electric energy is stored by windmills. Aviation and television are in operation, but they still share honors with bridle-paths, carriages, and bicycles; an incongruity which Mr. Astor shares with Mr. Wells and others.

Such are some of the lesser lights in the vast Utopian firmament, which in spite of their dim and wavering glow nevertheless manage to emit a sparkle of idea or ingenuity. These gleams, together with the brighter and the duller ones, shine from all points of the compass except the east. In nationality Utopia is entirely an occidental product. The three or four ancient Greeks were followed geographically by about as many modern Italians. The Teutons, counting Germans, Dutch, Austrians and Scandinavians, muster about a dozen. The French and the Americans each double that number, and the English top the list with two and a half dozen.

As to chronology, the increasing momentum of the Utopian advance is shown by the fact that the eighteenth century produced as many as the sixteenth and seventeenth together, that the nineteenth almost tripled that number, and that the twentieth so far—not yet a third gone—has almost as many as the nineteenth.

Whether the quality is keeping pace with the quantity is another matter. Excellence is rare in any age or clime. The editor of a current liberal journal testifies that his official mail is flooded with volunteered Utopian projects, mostly worthless.

But if there is a ludicrous pathos in the spectacle of these eager litters destined to be drowned at birth like so many superfluous kittens, there is a compensating encouragement in the evidence from other sources that formulated idealism is coming more and more into favor.

Any qualitative ranking of the Utopias we already have is too difficult and dubious to be worth the effort. No comparative estimate is possible when the standards of comparison are so numerous, subjective, and altogether slippery. Not only is one man's paradise another man's purgatory or worse, but among these constellations a star of the first magnitude in form may be fourth in content, and vice versa. All that may be ventured is the proportionate rating, and that shows an uneven balance indeed. Of the nearly ten dozen titles on the Utopian list scarcely three dozen could pass the main tests of comprehensiveness, symmetrical framework, concrete convincing drama, and fundamental seriousness of purpose. The majority are either fragmentary or lop-sided or fanatic or vague or conceived in skepticism rather than faith. Even so, each one listed has one feature or another so Utopian as to warrant its inclusion.

It may be, as one of our critics has said, that Utopias fall between two stools by being "too inartistic to be literature and too unscientific to be statesmanship," but they may at least claim to be kith to the one and kin to the other. And as such, for all the shoddy artistry of some and the shallow science of others, they deserve to be given anyway the left hand of fellowship. Whether or not the truly Utopian Utopia ever will be written, or remain as mythical as the Great American Novel, all these fractional contributions may be added up into a unit of considerable point and value.

Meanwhile we have Bertrand Russell's word for it that our hopes of downing poverty and disease, and concentrating on constructive arts and sciences appear Utopian simply by reason of our set yet plastic psychology. He announces that "The road to Utopia is clear; it lies partly through politics and partly through changes in the individual." That is to say, the materials of its mapping and building are partly humanitarian and partly humanistic. And the philosopher's conclusion that to find this road and travel it is merely a matter of physical and mental health may well be capped with the reminder that no road can be travelled or even found until it is made. Our large and busy gang of surveyors and engineers have by no means achieved a Utopian highway but they have assembled enough materials to serve as preliminary equipment for the superior architects even now visible in the offing, and for their long train of successors whose practical idealism will be more and more capably bent toward converting the potential Eutopia into the actual.

To be a Utopian is at the worst a guileless eccentricity. To be a Eutopian is an urgent necessity if our wobbling old world is to be made simply safe. What it can be made safe for, will still be the question. A multitude of random guesses may sometime generate the right answer.

L'ENVOI

A.D. 2000

Without a doubt both you and I
Will be considered, by and by,
As very odd and very queer
By all the people living here.

The way we speak, the way we dress,
The pleasures of our idleness
They'll ridicule without restraint
And think us very, very quaint.

The things in which we pride ourselves
To the historian who delves
In early twentieth century
Will seem such empty vanity!

The way we struggle, fight, and strive,
The stratagems whereby we thrive,
The things we hope for and desire
Will not be what they most admire.

Odd and archaic we shall be;
They'll say we lived so curiously,
They'll wonder at our negligence
And why we hadn't better sense.

ELLWOOD HENDRICK
Preface to his *Percolator Papers*

(Reprinted by permission of Harpers)

INDEX

Adam, Paul (LETTRES DE MA-LAISIE), 102, 148, 157, 298.
Ajaonier (Fontenelle: HISTOIRE DES AJAOIENS), 67, 80, 101, 143, 161.
Altruria (Howells: A TRAVELLER FROM ALTRURIA. THE EYE OF THE NEEDLE), 61, 80, 102, 129, 132, 163, 191f., 221.
AMAZONIAN REPUBLIC (Savage), 169.
Ammon, M. (DAS EI DES KOLUMBUS), 261.
ANATOMY OF MELANCHOLY (Burton), 192.
Andreae, Johann (CHRISTIANOPOLIS), 64, 88f., 91, 110, 140, 159, 175, 177, 192, 282.
ARISTOKIA (Pezet), 226.
Aristophanes, 177, 186.
ARISTOPIA (Holford), 74, 298.
ARMATA (Erskine), 177.
Ashbee, C. R. (BUILDING OF THELEMA), 265.
Astor, J. J. (JOURNEY TO OTHER WORLDS), 306.
AVENTURES DE JACQUES SADEUR (Foigny), 117.

BACK TO METHUSELAH (Shaw), 166, 171.
Bacon, Francis (NEW ATLANTIS, Bensalem), 48, 64, 80, 90, 116, 127, 131, 139f., 168, 182, 254, 275, 281f.
Ballanche, P. S. (VILLE DES EXPIATIONS), 303.

Ballou, Aden (HOPEDALE), 262f.
Baxter, Richard (HOLY COMMONWEALTH), 141.
Bellamy, Edward (LOOKING BACKWARD. EQUALITY), 50, 73, 75ff., 96, 104ff., 143, 165, 203f., 207, 209, 213, 217, 219, 225, 227f., 249f., 260, 296, 300ff.
Bensalem (Bacon: NEW ATLANTIS), 80, 90, 116.
Benson, R. H. (DAWN OF ALL. LORD OF THE WORLD), 50, 80, 149, 186ff., 217, 282, 285.
Berington, Simon (MEMOIRES DE GAUDENCE DE LUCQUES, Mezzorania), 67, 143, 291.
Besant, Walter (INNER HOUSE), 228.
BEYOND HELL (McKenna), 303.
Bilz, F. E. (IN HUNDERT JAHREN), 157.
BIRTH OF FREEDOM (Salisbury), 104, 304.
Blatchford, Robert (SORCERY SHOP), 50, 76, 107, 122, 133, 163, 225, 260, 282, 285.
BRAVE NEW WORLD (Huxley), 193ff.
Bretonne (see Restif).
BROOK FARM (Hawthorne), 261.
Brugh, James (CESSARES), 291.
Bruzov, Valerius (REPUBLIK DES SUDKREUZES), 229.
Butler, Samuel (EREWHON), 183, 193.
BY AND BY (Maitland), 143, 171.

INDEX

Cabet, Étienne (VOYAGE EN ICARIE, Icaria), 72, 160, 257ff., 292f., 299.
CAESAR'S COLUMN (Donnelly), 80, 217.
Calejava (Gilbert: HISTOIRE DE CALEJAVA), 102.
Campanella, Thomas (CITY OF THE SUN), 64, 89, 106, 115, 131, 140, 157, 192, 221, 282.
Cantahar (Mondasse: L'EMPIRE DE CANTAHAR), 67, 117, 142, 159.
Centennius, Ralph (Pseud. for Ralph Peterborough: DOMINION IN 1983), 294.
CESSARES (Brugh), 291f.
Chambless, Edgar (ROADTOWN), 117.
Chavannes, Albert (FUTURE COMMONWEALTH), 305.
Christianopolis (Andreae: CHRISTIANOPOLIS), 88, 93, 102, 110, 115, 128, 132, 140, 154, 176, 282.
City of the Sun (Campanella: CITY OF THE SUN), 89, 106, 115, 129, 139, 154, 221, 283.
COLYMBIA (Dudgeon), 72, 118, 157.
COMING RACE (Lytton: Vrilya), 92, 166.
COMMONWEALTH OF OCEANA (Stubbe), 283.
Condorcet, M. J. (ESQUISSE D'UN TABLEAU HISTORIQUE), 301.
Cooper, J. F. (THE CRATER), 50, 72, 95, 118, 143, 281, 294.
Craig, Alexander (IONIA), 73, 161, 296.
Crater (Cooper: THE CRATER), 72, 95, 118, 143, 294.
Crescent Island (More: UTOPIA), 63, 102, 153.
CRITIAS (Plato), 137, 290.
CRUCIBLE ISLAND (Pallen), 230.

CRYSTAL AGE (Hudson), 168.
CYROPAEDIA (Xenophon), 51, 290.

DAWN OF ALL (Benson), 149, 188, 226.
DEMOCRACY—FALSE OF TRUE (Richmond), 133.
Diothas (Thiusen: THE DIOTHAS), 49, 96, 104, 111, 165, 303.
Disraeli, Benjamin (CAPTAIN POPANELLA), 178.
DREAM (Wells), 239.
DREAM CITY (Unitas), 103, 148, 164.

Ellis, G. A. (NEW BRITAIN), 107, 291.
Emerson, R. W., 262, 266.
EMPIRE OF THE NAIRS (Lawrence), 169.
ENGLISH REVOLUTION (Lazarus), 221, 298.
EQUALITY (Bellamy), 205.
EREWHON (Butler), 183, 193.
Erskine, Thomas (ARMATA), 177.
ERSTE MILLIARD (Ströbel), 205f.
Ervine, St. John, 248.
ETWAS SPÄTER (Laicus), 213ff.
EYE OF THE NEEDLE (Howells), 76, 192.

Fairchild, F. P. (STORY OF THE CITY OF WORKS), 74.
Fénelon, François (TELEMACHUS), 68, 117, 126, 128, 142, 192, 281, 290.
FIXED PERIOD (Trollope), 180ff.
Foigny, Gabriel de (AVENTURES DE JACQUES SADEUR), 48, 65, 117.
Follin, H. L. (LA REVOLUTION DU QUATRE SEPTEMBRE), 287.
Fontenelle, Bernard de (HISTOIRE DES AJAOIENS), 67, 143.
Fourier, Joseph, 153, 260, 296, 299.

INDEX 313

Fox, Mary (NEW HOLLAND), 117, 291.
France, Anatole (WHITE STONE), 76, 94, 107, 117, 155, 165, 279, 281.
Francé, R. H. (PHOEBUS), 302.
France-Ville (Verne: FIVE HUNDRED MILLION), 155.
Freeland (Hertzka: FREELAND), 49, 73, 102, 118, 129, 132, 164, 218, 254.

Gaston, Henry (MARS REVISITED), 169.
Geiseler, Ludwig (LOOKING BEYOND), 205.
GEYSERLAND (Hatfield), 301.
Gilbert, Claude (HISTOIRE DE CALEJAVA), 157.
Giles, Fayette (SHADOWS BEFORE), 219.
Gott, Samuel (NOVA SOLYMA), 91, 141.
Gregory, Owen (MECCANIA), 226f.

Haldane, Charlotte (MAN'S WORLD), 171, 293.
Hale, E. E. (MY VISIT TO SYBARIS), 75, 95, 155, 281, 297.
Halévy, Daniel (HISTOIRE DES QUATRE ANS), 184, 205, 301.
Hall, Joseph (MUNDUS ALTER ET IDEM), 177, 179.
HAPPY COLONY (Pemberton), 92, 293.
Harrington, James (OCEANA), 64, 67, 102, 125, 141, 282f., 290.
Haskell, Burnette (HOW KAWEAH FAILED), 263f.
Hauptmann, Gerhart (ISLAND OF THE GREAT MOTHER), 162, 168.
Hellenbach, L. B. (DIE INSEL MELLONTA), 106, 157f., 295.
Hendrick, Ellwood, 310.

Hertzka, Theodor (FREELAND. FREELAND REVISITED), 50, 73, 218, 254ff., 260.
Holford, Castello (ARISTOPIA), 74, 298.
HOMME VOLANT (Restif: Megapatagonia), 157, 284.
House, Edward (PHILIP DRU), 74, 282, 287.
HOW WE BROUGHT ABOUT THE REVOLUTION (Petaud and Pouget), 103, 301.
Howells, W. D. (EYE OF THE NEEDLE, TRAVELLER FROM ALTRURIA), 76, 107, 110, 155, 191, 281, 291.
Hudson, W. H. (CRYSTAL AGE), 168, 281.
Huxley, Aldous (BRAVE NEW WORLD), 193ff.
Huxley, Julian, 201.
Hythloday, Raphael (More: UTOPIA), 42, 63, 87, 127.

Icaria (Cabet: VOYAGE EN ICARIE), 72, 102, 129, 257f., 292, 299.
IN THE DAYS OF THE COMET (Wells), 239.
INNER HOUSE (Besant), 228.
Intermere (Taylor: INTERMERE), 102, 111, 164.
Ionia (Craig: IONIA), 73, 103, 118, 132, 296.
IRDISCHE PARADIES (Merejkowski), 94f., 118, 162, 288.
IRON HEEL (London), 204, 224.
ISLES OF WISDOM (Moszkowski), 71, 182, 189.

Jaeger, M. (QUESTION MARK), 50, 81, 111, 119, 149, 243, 249.
JAPANESE UTOPIA (Magnus), 71, 182.
Jowett, Benjamin, 279.

INDEX

Kalomera (Saunders: KALOMERA), 80, 103, 111, 118, 144, 155, 164.
KENNEQUAHAIR (McCrib), 178.

Laicus, Philip (Pseud. for Philip Wasserburg: ETWAS SPÄTER), 213ff.
Lamartine, Alphonse de, 297.
L'AN DEUX MILLE (Restif de la Bretonne), 284.
Lane, William, 260.
L'ANNO TRE MILLE (Mantegazza), 71.
LAST DAYS OF THE REPUBLIC (Dooner), 208.
LAST OF MY RACE (Tayler), 49.
Lazarus, Henry (ENGLISH REVOLUTION), 221, 298.
Lee, Vernon, 249, 274.
Lewis, George, 275.
L'ILE DE NAUDELAY (Anon.), 192.
Limanora (Sweven: THE ISLAND OF PROGRESS), 72ff., 119, 130, 133, 144, 146, 153, 183, 190f., 205, 233, 288, 303.
London, Jack (IRON HEEL), 204, 224.
LOOKING BACKWARD (Bellamy), 73, 76, 202ff., 219, 223, 228, 260, 296.
LOOKING BEYOND (Geiseler), 205, 208.
LOOKING FORWARD (Michaelis), 205, 218.
LOOKING FURTHER BACKWARD (Vinton), 207ff.
LOOKING WITHIN (Roberts), 219ff.
LORD OF THE WORLD (Benson), 149, 186, 217.
LYCURGUS (Plutarch), 51, 91, 290.
Lynd, Robert, 276, 279f.
Lytton, Bulwer (COMING RACE), 69, 92, 103, 111, 129, 133, 143, 166, 198, 242, 281.

MACARIA (Stiblimus), 64.
McKenna, Stephen (BEYOND HELL), 303.
MacLeish, Archibald, 277.
Madariaga, Salvator (SACRED GIRAFFE), 172.
Maitland, Edward (BY AND BY), 143, 171.
Mallock, N. H. (NEW REPUBLIC), 192.
MAN FROM MARS (Simpson), 103, 148, 305.
MAN'S WORLD (Haldane), 171, 293.
Mantegazza, Paolo (L'ANNO TRE MILLE), 71, 143, 171, 182.
Marquis, Don (ALMOST PERFECT STATE), 251.
Marshall, Archibald (UPSIDONIA), 180.
Masson, Émile (UTOPIE DES ÎLES BIENHEUREUSES), 302.
MASTER BEAST (Newte), 224.
MEANWHILE (Wells), 250.
MECCANIA (Gregory), 226f.
Megapatagonia (Restif: HOMME VOLANT), 67, 102, 116, 131, 133, 143, 163, 284.
MEN LIKE GODS (Wells), 240ff.
Mercier, L. S. (L'AN 2440. THE YEAR 2500), 50, 68, 94, 117, 143, 282ff.
Mercury (Anon.: MONDE DE MERCURE), 101, 133, 143, 166.
Merejkowski, Dmitri (IRDISCHE PARADIES), 94f., 101, 118, 129, 147, 162, 282, 288.
Mezzorania (Berington: GAUDENTIO DI LUCCA), 67, 143, 163.
Michaelis, Richard (LOOKING FORWARD), 205, 218f.
MODERN UTOPIA (Wells), 240, 244, 250, 293.
Mondasse, Varennes de (L'EMPIRE DE CANTAHAR), 67, 142, 159.

INDEX

More, Thomas (UTOPIA), 41f., 52, 63, 88, 101, 103, 107, 115, 127, 131f., 137, 140, 153, 155, 159, 175, 201, 244, 281.
Morelly, M. (CODE DE LA NATURE), 109.
Morgan, J. M. (REVOLT OF THE BEES), 179f.
Morris, William (NEWS FROM NOWHERE), 50, 76, 92, 94, 102, 105, 107, 133, 188, 240, 249, 281, 291.
Moszkowski, Alexander (ISLES OF WISDOM), 71, 182.
MR. EAST'S EXPERIENCES (Wilbrandt), 209.
Mueller, Ernst (RÜCKBLICK), 209, 212f.

NEUSTRIA (Thirion), 72, 94, 116, 259, 292f.
NEW ATLANTIS (Bacon: Bensalem), 91, 128, 168, 182, 192, 254.
NEW BRITAIN (Ellis), 80, 155, 291.
NEW COLUMBIA (Tangent), 278.
NEW GULLIVER (Pain), 224f.
NEW HOLLAND (Fox), 70, 117, 291.
NEWAERA (Herbert), 225, 285.
NEWS FROM NOWHERE (Morris), 76.
NIELS KLIM (Holberg), 180.
NINETY-SIX (Rosewater), 221, 294.
NOUVELLE CYROPAEDIE (Anon.), 192.
NOVA SOLYMA (Gott), 91.

OCEANA (Harrington), 49, 66, 126, 141, 283, 290.
Ollivant, Alfred (TOMORROW), 105, 108, 183.
OPHIR (Anon.), 65, 90f., 128, 140, 163f.
Owen, Robert, 261f.

Pain, Barry (NEW GULLIVER), 224f.
Pallen, Condé (CRUCIBLE ISLAND), 230.
Pemberton, Robert (HAPPY COLONY), 92, 293.
PENGUIN ISLAND (Anatole France), 186.
Pezet, A. W. (ARISTOKIA), 226.
PHILIP DRU (House), 74, 287.
Plato (REPUBLIC: Socrates), 48, 50, 62, 86, 101, 128, 137, 153, 159, 175, 192, 244, 271, 281, 290, 296.
Plutarch (LYCURGUS), 51, 62, 281, 290.

QUESTION MARK (Jaeger), 81, 119, 149, 249.

REIGN OF GEORGE VI (Anon.), 178.
REPUBLIC (Plato), 101, 244, 290.
Restif de la Bretonne, N. A. E. (HOMME VOLANT. L'AN DEUX MILLE. Megapatagonia), 67, 116, 143, 153, 157, 282, 284.
REVOLT OF THE BEES (Morgan), 179.
RIALLARO (Sweven: ARCHIPELAGO OF EXILES), 71f., 145, 189f., 288.
Richter, Eugene (ZUKUNFTBILDER), 208f.
Roberts, J. W. (LOOKING WITHIN), 219ff.
Rosewater, Frank (DOOMED. NINETY-SIX), 48, 74, 107, 164, 221, 294.
Rossi, Giovanni (UTOPIE UND EXPERIMENT), 107, 253.
RÜCKBLICK (Mueller), 209.
Ruskin, John, 202.
Russell, Bertrand, 309.

SACRED GIRAFFE (Madariaga), 172.
Salisbury, H. B. (BIRTH OF FREE-
DOM), 103f., 304.
Saunders, W. J. (KALOMERA), 107,
118, 144, 155.
Savage, Timothy (AMAZONIAN RE-
PUBLIC), 169.
SCARLET EMPIRE (Perry), 223.
Schindler, Solomon (YOUNG WEST),
96, 205.
Scudder, Vida, 279.
Shaw, Bernard (BACK TO METHU-
SELAH), 49, 166, 171.
Sherman, Stuart, 248.
Simpson, William (MAN FROM
MARS), 103, 148, 305.
SKYDROMEDIA (LeGrand), 290.
Socrates (see Plato).
SONNENSTADT (Vetsch), 103, 129.
SORCERY SHOP (Blatchford), 76,
163, 225, 285.
Spence, Thomas (SPENSONIA), 69,
282, 284.
Stanley, William (CASE OF THEO-
DORE FOX), 50, 77f., 93, 103,
119, 148, 155, 161.
STORY OF THE TIME TO COME
(Wells), 236.
Sweven, Godfrey (Pseud. for John
Macmillan Brown: LIMANORA.
RIALLERO), 71ff., 129, 133, 144,
153, 183, 189, 282, 288.
Swift, Jonathan (LAPUTA. HOUYN-
MNMS), 177.
Swift, Morrison (HORROBOOS), 177,
233.
Sybaris (Hale: MY VISIT TO
SYBARIS), 75, 95f., 118, 155, 297.

Tardé, Gabriel (UNDERGROUND
MAN), 129, 133, 282, 286.
Taylor, William (INTERMERE), 164.
Telemachus, (Fénelon: TÉLÉ-
MAQUE), 68, 117, 142, 192, 290.

Thirion, Émile (NEUSTRIA), 72, 94,
116, 259, 292f.
Thiusen, Ismar (DIOTHAS), 50, 72,
80, 96, 107, 165, 303.
TIME MACHINE (Wells), 237.
TOMORROW (Ollivant), 105, 183.
Trollope, Anthony (FIXED PERIOD),
180ff.

UCHRONIE (Renouvier), 302.
UNDERGROUND MAN (Tardé), 286.
Unitas (DREAM CITY), 103, 148.
UTOPIA FOUND (Mangin), 178.
UTOPIE UND EXPERIMENT (Rossi),
253.

Vairasse, Denis d'Alais (HISTOIRE
DES SEVERAMBES, Sevarites), 48,
65, 153.
Verne, Jules (FIVE HUNDRED MIL-
LION OF THE BEGUM), 155, 294.
Vinton, Arthur (LOOKING FURTHER
BACKWARD), 207f., 217.
VISIT TO FREELAND (Hertzka), 257.
VOICE FROM POSTERITY (Hay), 168.
Voltaire, François, 295.
Vrilya (Lytton: COMING RACE),
103, 111, 119, 130, 133, 143,
165f., 224, 242.

WE (Zamiatin), 193, 232.
Wells, H. G. (COMET. DREAM.
MEN LIKE GODS. MODERN
UTOPIA. TIME MACHINE), 50,
74ff., 80, 111, 235f., 238ff., 281,
293, 306f.
WHEN THE SLEEPER WAKES
(Wells), 236.
WHITE STONE (Anatole France),
76, 186.
Wiggam, A. E., 201, 276.
Wilbrandt, Konrad (MR. EAST'S EX-
PERIENCES), 209f.
Wilde, Oscar, 279.

WORK (ZOLA: TRAVAIL), 76, 261, 292.
WORLD SET FREE (Wells), 239.

Xenophon (CYROPAEDIA), 51, 62, 281, 290.

YOUNG WEST (Schindler), 205, 221.

Zamiatin, Eugene (WE), 193, 232.
Zola, Émile (WORK), 50, 76, 116, 261, 281, 292.
ZUKUNFTBILDER (Richter), 208f.